Changes in the Workweek of Fixed Capital

Changes in the Workweek of Fixed Capital

U.S. Manufacturing, 1929 to 1976

Murray F. Foss

American Enterprise Institute for Public Policy Research
Washington and London

Murray F. Foss, a visiting scholar at the American Enterprise Institute, has served as a senior research associate at the National Bureau of Economic Research in Washington and, from 1969 to 1975, as a senior staff economist with the Council of Economic Advisers. Earlier, he was editor of the *Survey of Current Business* and chief of the Current Business Analysis Division of the Bureau of Economic Analysis in the Department of Commerce.

Library of Congress Cataloging in Publication Data

Foss, Murray.
  Changes in the workweek of fixed capital.

  (AEI studies ; 309)
  Bibliography: p.
  1. Industrial equipment—United States—Utilization.
2. Capital. 3. Hours of labor—United States.
I. Title. II. Series: American Enterprise Institute for
Public Policy Research. AEI studies ; 309.
HD39.3.F67   338.4'5   80-28063
ISBN 0-8447-3422-5
ISBN 0-8447-3423-3 (pbk.)

AEI studies 309

Printed in the United States of America

Contents

Acknowledgments

This study was aided by a grant from the National Science Foundation and was given further support by the Bureau of the Census. I am grateful to Shirley Kallek, associate director for economic fields in the Census Bureau, for her help. During the course of the study numerous individuals provided assistance, especially my research assistant Robert Dubman. Help with the basic data, including the sample selection, estimation procedure, and tabulation of the 1929 census returns, was provided by several employees of the Census Bureau, among them Wayne McCaughey, chief of the Special Projects Branch of the Industry Division, who was in charge of the project at the bureau. In addition, special mention should be made of Milton Eisen, Arthur Horowitz, Mary Jenkins, Edward Robinson, Linda Schlueter, Jay Waite, and Jack Wasil. Criticisms of the manuscript and suggestions were made by Barry Chiswick, Edward Denison, William Fellner, Thomas Johnson, Marvin Kosters, Mickey Levy, Martin Marimont, and Milton Moss. I alone am responsible for errors and shortcomings that remain.

1
Introduction

The average worker works a much shorter week now than he did fifty years ago, but what can be said of the workweek of fixed capital—factories, warehouses, and the like—over this period? This study examines the change in the number of hours worked by manufacturing plants from 1929 to 1976. Information of this kind has significance for analyzing the growth of output, inputs, and of productivity over the long run; yet comprehensive statistics on hours worked by plants have never before been available for economic analysis.

This study is part of a larger investigation of changes in capital hours and their long-term significance. The study begins with a brief discussion of a fairly recent controversy involving the role of capital hours in growth accounting. Chapter 2 presents Census Bureau data on weekly plant hours for 1929 and 1976 and shows how an adjustment for average plant hours over the same forty-seven-year span might alter existing measures of changes in capital stocks and capital-output ratios. It also shows how changes in weekly plant hours are related to changes in total factor productivity by major industry. It concludes with a presentation of more detailed breakdowns of the data for 1929 and 1976, partly for the regression analysis that follows.

Chapter 3 analyzes factors accounting for changes in weekly plant hours over the span of almost half a century. The general approach has been to analyze industry variations on a cross-sectional basis—separately for 1929 and 1976—and then industry changes over time. The unit of observation is the detailed industry, for which some eighty-five to ninety-five industries or industry groups were available. The last chapter discusses some implications and an agenda for further research.

Findings

In the forty-seven years from 1929 to 1976, the average workweek of fixed capital in manufacturing increased by approximately 25 percent, or at an average annual rate of 0.47 percent. These figures would be a little higher if some allowance were made for the fact that plant hours may have been somewhat low in 1976 because of the business cycle. The overall rise reflects an increase in the number of hours worked per day as a result of increased shift work, partly offset by a decrease in the number of days worked per week. The rise occurred even though there was little or no change in the length of the plant workweek for that part of the stock of fixed capital that has typically worked around the clock. The plant workweek lengthened in most industries; decreases have been the exception. These reductions occurred even though average weekly hours worked by labor declined from a customary week of about fifty hours in 1929 to forty hours in 1976.

From 1929 to 1976, the gross stock of fixed capital in manufacturing (measured in constant 1972 prices) rose by 166 percent, or at an average annual rate of 2.10 percent. The average annual rise in weekly plant hours over this period was thus 22 percent of the average annual gross stock increase. The rise in average weekly plant hours provides a partial explanation for the pronounced drop—almost 45 percent—in the ratio of fixed capital to output in manufacturing from 1929 to 1976. The drop is about 30 percent after the rise in plant hours is accounted for.

In a growth accounting context, the rise in average weekly plant hours can be viewed in one of two ways. It means that the contribution of fixed capital to output growth in manufacturing has been greater than has previously been measured; or it means that the growth in total factor productivity, as that is now measured, reflects in part the effect of the rise in average weekly plant hours. With the major (two-digit) industry as a unit of observation, it was possible to observe a significant relationship between changes in average weekly plant hours and changes in total factor productivity over the forty-seven-year span from 1929 to 1976.

Several factors explain the rise in average weekly plant hours from 1929 to 1976. One is the increase in the capital intensity of production in most manufacturing industries and the attempt by business to economize on capital use under these circumstances. An aspect related to increased capital intensity is the increase in the importance of plants that work continuously through the year. Such plants now account for about 28 percent of manufacturing fixed capital, half again as large as the 1929 proportion.

2

Large plants (measured by value added) work the most hours per week. Industries in which plants and companies tend to be small and most output is produced in single-plant companies tend to work the fewest hours per week. On the assumption that many owners of small manufacturing businesses consider their presence in the plant vital to its proper management, this probably reflects a preference of such owners for leisure as against income. The decreased relative importance of small firms in manufacturing over the years has contributed to the lengthening of the plant workweek.

The need to pay labor a wage differential for working late shifts would ordinarily act to discourage the adoption of shift work. Such differentials are fairly common today, in contrast to the apparent situation before World War II. Although my statistical analysis did not find shift differentials significant in explaining average weekly plant hours, I believe that since the end of World War II the trend of shift differentials has fostered the adoption of extra shifts because the differentials have not kept pace with the rise of manufacturing wages. The influence of the differentials has probably been small, however, because they remain small in relation to wages generally.

Shift work or long average weekly plant hours used to be less evenly distributed among the major regions of the nation than is the case today. The change is more than just a mix effect. In 1929 plants operating two or more shifts per day were relatively more common in the South and West than in the Northeast and North Central regions. Possibly this reflected the relative scarcity of capital in the South and West at that time.

Firms or industries in which labor worked long weekly hours in 1929 were faced with large overtime bills as a result of the federal wage-hour law. These industries acted in response to the strong incentives to adopt or increase shift work.

The Growth Accounting Background

In accounting for the long-term growth of real output in the U.S. economy, the importance of fixed capital inputs has been a subject of controversy, especially since the appearance of studies by investigators such as Moses Abramovitz, Edward Denison, Solomon Fabricant, John Kendrick, and Robert Solow in the 1950s and early 1960s. One source of controversy has revolved around the measurement of capital input, in particular whether an input measured by the change in a constant dollar stock of capital in place should be adjusted also for the long-term increase in hours worked per unit of capital. The main protagonists in what could be called the capital utilization controversy that was carried on from about the mid-1960s to the early

3

1970s were Denison, on the one hand, and Dale Jorgenson and various collaborators, on the other.

The capital utilization controversy was part of a broader debate about the sources of growth in the United States. Two key conclusions of the studies mentioned were that (1) the importance of fixed capital in accounting for growth in a national income accounting framework has been considerable but smaller than commonly thought, and (2) the portion of growth accounted for by output per unit of input (or total factor productivity, or "the residual") has been comparatively large. For example, in his first study of the sources of economic growth in the United States, Denison attributed one-third of the growth in real national income from 1929 to 1957 to the growth in total factor productivity and two-thirds to the growth in factor inputs—labor, land, and capital.[1] The growth of capital accounted for 15 percent of income growth over this period. In his pioneering work on the sources of economic growth in the United States, Denison explained the long-run growth of total factor productivity by a number of influences, such as economies of scale, the shift of resources out of agriculture, and advances in knowledge. Quantifying the effects of all these influences on productivity growth has been and remains a difficult task, and despite Denison's trail-blazing efforts, many economists still view the residual as a measure of economists' ignorance of the causes of growth.

In 1967 the Denison findings were criticized on both theoretical and statistical grounds by Jorgenson and Griliches, who offered an alternative set of estimates of the sources of growth in the United States.[2] In their calculations Jorgenson and Griliches assigned a greatly reduced role to productivity growth and a much increased role to the growth of factor inputs, in particular to the input of fixed capital. In their view the importance of fixed capital was understated for a number of reasons, one of the most significant of which was the failure of Denison to allow for the long-term growth in the relative utilization of the capital stock.

For evidence of increased utilization, Jorgenson and Griliches extended the findings of a 1963 article by Murray Foss, which compared the relative utilization of capital equipment in the post–World War II period with utilization before the Great Depression.[3] His

---

[1] Edward F. Denison, *The Sources of Economic Growth in the United States and the Alternatives before Us*, Committee for Economic Development Supplementary Paper No. 13 (New York, 1962).

[2] Dale W. Jorgenson and Zvi Griliches, "The Explanation of Productivity Change," *Review of Economic Studies*, vol. 34, no. 99 (July 1967), pp. 249-83.

[3] Murray F. Foss, "The Utilization of Capital Equipment," *Survey of Current Business*, vol. 43, no. 6 (June 1963), pp. 8-16.

4

principal findings were as follows: (1) From 1929 to the high employment years of the mid-1950s, hours worked per year per unit of equipment in manufacturing rose by approximately one-half. (2) Other data pertaining to mining equipment, generating equipment in electric utilities, railroad locomotives, and textile machinery also showed increased utilization over this period. (3) No attempt was made to explain the rise in relative utilization of equipment. The article suggested, however, that increased use of multiple shifts, a trend toward continuously operated industries as a result of technological change, and more efficient use of machinery were some of the influences underlying the rise in relative utilization. (4) The article took no stand on how the main findings should be incorporated into growth accounting but suggested two possibilities: (a) Increased long-run utilization of equipment could signify that the contribution of fixed capital to output growth was greater and the importance of productivity correspondingly less than had been indicated in growth analysis; this followed from the fact that the change in fixed capital was typically measured by the change of a constant dollar series of capital in place without any adjustment for changed utilization. (b) The rise in hours worked by capital equipment could be viewed not as a rise in capital input but as the result of certain forces contributing to the long-run increase in total factor productivity, such as increased efficiency in the use of machinery by business. The article made extensive use of census statistics on electric power consumption and on electric motors in place in manufacturing plants. Factories have long used electric motors to run most of the power-driven equipment employed in production.

In his rebuttal, Denison criticized Jorgenson and Griliches on several counts, especially for what he saw as their inadequate consideration of the conceptual problems underlying the long-run changes in the utilization of capital.[4] In particular he took issue with their notion that if there is no adjustment to capital stock for increased utilization, the growth of total factor productivity must be overstated. In his view it was conceivable that all of the long-run rise in equipment utilization was already reflected in labor and capital inputs. For example, to the extent that businessmen purchase more reliable and—on that account—more expensive machinery, the value of the capital stock will be increased, and productivity will be unaffected. Machines may work longer hours over the long run because of reduced downtime, which in turn may reflect increased use of inventories of

[4] Edward F. Denison, "Some Major Issues in Productivity Analysis: An Examination of Estimates by Jorgenson and Griliches" and "Final Comments," *Survey of Current Business*, vol. 52, no. 5 (May 1972), part II.

spare parts by maintenance workers. The former changes would mean greater labor input; the latter, greater inventory (capital) input. Productivity need not be affected. Denison noted that among the possible reasons for a rise in hours worked by capital over the long run there were two that might contribute to the rise in productivity as he measured it: increased shift work and advances in management knowledge. An example of the latter would be a reduction of seasonal peaks in production. This would reduce the need for standby equipment and permit a more intensive use of existing equipment through the year.

In *Why Growth Rates Differ*, Denison analyzed the growth in shift work from 1950 to 1962 in the United States as revealed in statistics on employment by shift in manufacturing.[5] Since these figures showed no change in the proportion of workers employed on late shifts during the period under consideration, he gave a value of zero to changes in the importance of shift work as a factor accounting for growth.

Jorgenson and Griliches conceded a number of points made by Denison, in particular that their utilization adjustment was given too much weight because it was applied to housing and inventories as well as to all business fixed capital. Partly because of this, there was a narrowing between their position and that of Denison on the relative roles of factor inputs and productivity in accounting for growth. Differences with Denison remained, however. In their view there was no compelling evidence that rising equipment utilization over time was already reflected in measured factor inputs. They regarded the utilization adjustment as an interesting one and, as a source of growth, an element of potential importance applicable to plant as well as to equipment. They also felt it important to explain why relative utilization had increased, although in their opinion whether one treated the rise in relative utilization as capital input or as part of total factor productivity was not important. (Denison would not disagree with this classification problem so long as measurements do not involve duplication.)

In his 1974 study, Denison did not explicitly measure change in annual hours worked by capital.[6] He restated the position he took initially in criticizing Jorgenson and Griliches: that in the long run such changes in relative utilization as may occur are manifestations of elements already measured in his framework, with the possible

[5] Edward F. Denison, *Why Growth Rates Differ* (Washington, D.C.: Brookings Institution, 1967).

[6] Edward F. Denison, *Accounting for United States Economic Growth 1929-1969* (Washington, D.C.: Brookings Institution, 1974).

exception of the "prevalence of shift work when industry weights are held constant."

Jorgenson dropped the capital utilization adjustment in his more recent studies of total factor productivity growth in collaboration with Christensen.[7] In a paper presented in a conference of the National Bureau of Economic Research at Williamsburg in 1975, however, Jorgenson and Frank Gollop described their use of fuel and power (intermediate inputs) as implicit measures of capital utilization.[8] Some foreign investigators have explicitly used energy consumption as a proxy for capital utilization.

Census Data

The treatment of the long-term increase in capital utilization in the United States has remained an unresolved problem mainly because data have been lacking. Past studies did not seem to offer much hope for a solution. For example, taking the approach that uses census electricity consumption and motor data would require new statistics not available or presently planned. Although the Census Bureau has collected power consumption statistics for many years, since 1962 it has not collected horsepower statistics, a very old time series dating back to the nineteenth century. Even if such data were available, it would still be necessary to collect up-to-date information on the purposes of electric power consumption in manufacturing plants. The last such study applied to 1945. It found that power was used in manufacturing mainly for driving motors but also for lighting and other purposes. We do not know whether and to what extent the distribution of power use within industries has changed since then. Finally, the electricity-horsepower data do not indicate why there has been an increase in hours worked by equipment over the period observed. They do not provide the basis for an unequivocal utilization adjustment that can be used with data on capital stocks in place in a growth accounting framework.

---

[7] Laurits R. Christensen and Dale W. Jorgenson, "The Measurement of U.S. Real Capital Input," *Review of Income and Wealth,* series 15, no. 4 (December 1969), pp. 293-320; "U.S. Real Product and Real Factor Input, 1929-1967," *Review of Income and Wealth,* series 16, no. 1 (March 1970), pp 19-50; and "Measuring the Performance of the Private Sector of the U.S. Economy, 1929-1969," in Milton Moss, ed., *Measuring Economic and Social Performance* (New York: Columbia University Press for National Bureau of Economic Research, 1973).

[8] Frank M. Gollop and Dale W. Jorgenson, "U.S. Productivity Growth by Industry, 1947-73," in John W. Kendrick and Beatrice N. Vaccara, eds., *New Developments in Productivity Measurement and Analysis* (Chicago: University of Chicago Press for National Bureau of Economic Research, 1980).

TABLE 1

Average Number of Shifts, Days per Week, Hours per Day, and Hours per Week of Actual Plant Operations, All Manufacturing, Fourth Quarters 1973–1977

	1973	1974	1975	1976	1977
Average number of shifts	2.1	1.8	1.9	1.9	1.9
Average days per week	5.4	5.2	5.4	5.3	5.4
Average hours per day	16.5	14.7	15.2	15.5	15.8
Average hours per week	89	76	82	82	85

Source: U.S. Department of Commerce, Bureau of the Census, *Survey of Plant Capacity*, MQ-C, 1973, 1974, 1975, 1976, and 1977. Reflects use of employment weights.

Important new information has become available from a new sample survey undertaken by the Census Bureau. Starting in late 1975 as part of a survey of capacity utilization requested by the Federal Reserve Board, the bureau began to publish statistics on manufacturing shift operations and on daily and weekly hours worked by plants. The first survey covered manufacturing activity in the fourth quarter of 1973. Similar surveys have been conducted each year since then, the fourth quarter of 1977 being the latest published (early 1981).[9]

The new survey, designed to represent all U.S. manufacturing, has asked manufacturing plants to indicate hours operated per day and days per week as well as shifts per day. Information is requested for both actual and capacity operations. Combining plants with employment weights, the Census Bureau has found that manufacturing plants operate approximately two shifts of about forty hours each. In the boom conditions prevailing in the fourth quarter of 1973, plants worked an average of eighty-nine hours per week. In the fourth quarter of 1974, when the recession was under way, average hours per week had fallen to seventy-six, but since then they have made a partial recovery. These are aggregate figures that include the effects of changing industry mix over the business cycle. Table 1 shows for all manufacturing the number of shifts per day, hours worked per day, days worked per week, and hours worked per week for each of the surveys conducted so far. Table 2 shows for the fourth quarter of 1976 similar information broken down by two-digit industries. The questionnaire and instructions are included in appendix A, which is followed by Census Bureau material on sampling, response rates, and

---

[9] See appendix C for further detail.

TABLE 2

AVERAGE NUMBER OF SHIFTS PER DAY, DAYS PER WEEK, HOURS PER DAY,
AND HOURS PER WEEK OF ACTUAL PLANT OPERATIONS, BY INDUSTRY,
FOURTH QUARTER 1976

	Shifts/day	Days/week	Hours/day	Hours/week
Total manufacturing	1.9	5.3	15.5	82
Nondurable	2.0	5.4	15.9	86
Food	1.8	5.2	14.4	75
Tobacco	2.3	5.0	18.2	91
Textiles	2.6	5.3	20.8	110
Apparel	1.1	5.0	8.5	42
Paper	2.5	5.7	20.1	115
Printing and publishing	1.9	5.6	14.7	82
Chemicals	2.3	6.0	18.7	112
Petroleum	2.7	6.5	21.5	140
Rubber	2.5	5.4	20.0	108
Leather	1.1	5.0	8.9	44
Durable	1.8	5.3	15.3	81
Lumber	1.4	5.1	11.4	58
Furniture	1.2	5.0	10.2	51
Stone, clay, and glass	2.1	5.7	17.1	98
Primary metals	2.5	5.9	20.1	119
Fabricated metals	1.8	5.2	14.4	75
Machinery	1.9	5.2	15.3	80
Electrical machinery	1.8	5.1	14.4	73
Transportation equipment	1.9	5.2	16.8	87
Instruments	1.6	5.2	13.2	69
Miscellaneous	1.4	5.1	11.2	57

SOURCE: Bureau of the Census, *Survey of Plant Capacity*, 1977, p. 18. Reflects use of employment weights. Hours per week calculated by author as product of industry average hours per day and industry average days per week.

estimating in appendix B. Appendix C has a discussion of some reporting problems and of surveys of employment by shift by the Bureau of Labor Statistics.

An examination of the figures reveals that extra shifts are the rule rather than the exception in U.S. manufacturing. A high degree of multiple-shift work shows up, not only in industries where shift work has traditionally been found, such as primary metals, petroleum, and paper, but also in many other industries, such as food, tobacco, and textiles. Only a handful of industries operate on a single shift or something close to it: apparel, lumber, furniture, and leather. Even in the fourth quarter of 1974, when manufacturing output was falling very rapidly, multiple-shift operations in metal fabricating industries (industries 34 through 37) ranged from 1.6 to 1.9 shifts per day.

These findings may come as a surprise to the conventional view of U.S. manufacturing as being essentially one-shift except primarily for continuous industries such as petroleum refining. The persistence of the forty-hour week for labor may have encouraged the common view, but the average labor week and the average capital week can be quite different. A majority of employees work on the first shift, even in plants that operate continuously. These issues are discussed in appendix C.

If manufacturing now operates on a two-shift basis, what was the average length of the plant workweek in the past? For the years since 1959, Bureau of Labor Statistics data on employment by shift in metropolitan areas are available for all manufacturing combined. For the period before World War II, however, it is safe to say that no comprehensive information of this kind has been published for the United States, except for ad hoc surveys of limited coverage. For example, a study made by an engineering group in 1922 identified nearly forty "continuous" industries employing 500,000 to 1 million persons, or roughly 5 to 10 percent of total manufacturing employment.[10] On the basis of the very limited information available concerning past practice, it was my belief that before World War II most American industry operated on a one-shift basis except for continuous industries and a few other well-known cases. This meant that if one went back in time, skipping over the depression years to 1929, a year of high employment, one would find that plants on average were working a much shorter week than they are today, even though the standard workweek of the individual worker fifty years ago was greater than today's forty-hour week. But there was a dearth of solid information to back this up.

Indeed, the phenomenon of multiple-shift work has received little attention from economists until fairly recently. It is interesting that in the United States, where shift work is common, economic research on shift work and capital utilization has been extremely limited, although such investigators of U.S. growth and productivity as Moses Abramovitz and Solomon Fabricant noted the lack of information on shift work many years ago. In discussing the growth of capital from 1870 to the 1950s, Abramovitz stated:

---

[10] American Engineering Council, *The Twelve-Hour Shift in Industry* (New York: E. P. Dutton, 1922).

Our figures [capital stock estimates by Goldsmith and Kuznets] make no allowance for changes in the service hours of capital comparable with that of labor. There is no statistical basis for such an adjustment. The decline in labor hours is not a reliable indication since capital is often operated on multiple shifts or even continuously. It is not clear whether such practices have grown or declined.[11]

In 1956 Charles Schultze surmised that the secular decline in the workweek of labor was partly mirrored in a decline in hours worked by capital. He had no special data but estimated that from 1900 to the mid-1950s two-thirds of the decline in labor hours per week was reflected in a decline in the workweek of capital.[12] In his study of long-term changes in national income since 1870, Kuznets attached some validity to the argument that a decline in the workweek of labor was accompanied by a similar decline in the workweek of capital; but, citing the importance of continuous industries, he expressed the opinion that "the decline, if any, in working hours per unit of capital must be much smaller than in working hours per member of the labor force."[13] Allan Cartter felt that the trend toward a shorter labor week was offset by more intensive use of capital.[14]

In the middle 1950s, Robin Marris was starting on his pioneering analysis of multiple-shift work, which was published in 1964.[15] Nicholas Georgescu-Roegen in the Ely Lecture in New York in 1969 deplored the failure of economists to take account of factory working time in production functions. Finding so many theoretical deficiencies in production function analysis, he was not surprised that the "most sophisticated statistical agencies . . . have felt no need to include it [shift data] in their usual collections."[16]

---

[11] Moses Abramovitz, *Resource and Output Trends in the United States since 1870*, National Bureau of Economic Research, Occasional Paper 42 (New York, 1956), p. 10.

[12] Charles L. Schultze, "Some Effects of Changes in Working Hours on Investment, Output, and Real Wages," a paper presented at the Business and Economic Statistics Section, American Statistical Association Convention, 1956. Schultze subsequently felt that he had overstated the decline in capital hours.

[13] Simon Kuznets, *Capital in the American Economy: Its Formation and Financing* (Princeton, N.J.: Princeton University Press for the National Bureau of Economic Research, 1961), p. 80.

[14] Allan Cartter, *Proceedings of Ninth Annual Meeting, Industrial Relations Research Association*, 1956, pp. 224-27.

[15] Robin Marris, *The Economics of Capital Utilization* (Cambridge: Cambridge University Press, 1964).

[16] Nicholas Georgescu-Roegen, "The Economics of Production," *American Economic Review*, vol. 60, no. 2 (May 1970), p. 9.

TABLE 3

Hours per Week, Hours per Day, Days per Week, and Shifts per Day Operated by Manufacturing Plants, 1929

	Shifts/day	Days/week[a]	Hours/day	Hours/week
Food	1.3	5.9	11.8	70.3
Tobacco	1.0	5.7	8.8	50.0
Textiles	1.3	5.8	11.3	65.3
Apparel	1.0	5.5	8.3	45.7
Lumber	1.1	5.5	10.3	56.4
Furniture	1.0	5.6	9.0	50.3
Paper	2.0	5.7	17.0	97.1
Printing and publishing	1.3	6.0	10.5	62.8
Chemicals	1.8	6.4	15.1	95.9
Petroleum	2.9	6.8	22.8	154.3
Rubber	2.1	5.7	17.6	101.1
Leather	1.0	5.3	9.2	48.7
Stone, clay, and glass	1.6	6.0	13.2	79.3
Primary metals	2.4	6.1	18.8	115.2
Fabricated metals	1.1	5.6	9.8	54.5
Machinery	1.1	5.6	9.9	55.3
Electrical machinery	1.0	5.6	8.8	49.2
Transportation equipment	1.2	5.3	11.4	60.6
Instruments	1.1	5.7	9.2	52.2
Miscellaneous	1.0	5.6	8.7	48.6
Total manufacturing	1.3	5.8	11.5	66.5

[a] Hours per week divided by hours per day for total and each industry. Plant days per week were not reported *directly* on 1929 schedule.

Source: Basic data come from sample drawn from 1929 Census of Manufactures and blown up to universe totals with employment weights.

The major contribution of this study is the publication of information on weekly plant hours worked by manufacturing plants in 1929 for comparison with findings for recent years. What is unusual about the 1929 information is that it comes from the 1929 Census of Manufactures and reflects answers to a set of questions virtually identical with the questions used in the survey undertaken by the Census Bureau in the 1970s. Because of cost considerations, it was necessary to take a probability sample of the 1929 returns. The sampling plan used for 1929 is described in appendix D along with the schedule and instructions.[17]

Table 3 shows basic data for 1929 by two-digit industry. Extrapolations from sample to universe within industries and for all manufacturing reflect the use of wage-earner employment weights. Industry classifications for 1929 have been modified for greater conformity to 1972 classifications. See appendix F.

---

[17] A few words about the discovery of the 1929 reports may be of interest. The original questionnaire used by the Census Bureau for the 1929 Census of Manufactures shows a set of questions addressed to shift work and plant hours operated per day and per week. But tabulations of such data are nowhere to be found in any of the publications for that census. On the surface it seemed reasonable to infer that the answers had not been well reported. Initial inquiries by the author indicated that the 1929 schedules had been destroyed, but subsequent investigation revealed that they had been photographed and were available on microfilm. A spot-check by the Census Bureau over a broad array of industries revealed that respondents had indeed supplied the information to the Census Bureau. There are no records indicating why the information was not tabulated. The absence of a tabulation may have been due to the fact that this was the first time the question had been asked in a Census of Manufactures. To judge from the sample chosen for this study, however, reporting problems could not have been the reason, since they were few in number. Budgetary considerations were probably an important factor as the economy worsened in 1930 and 1931.

2

Changes in the Plant Workweek from 1929 to 1976 and Their Relation to Key Ratios

Changes in Average Weekly Plant Hours, 1929 to 1976

The average workweek of manufacturing plants increased from 1929 to 1976. Results for all manufacturing, given in table 4 on several bases, uniformly show increases. Two-digit industry results, given in the last column of table 5, show increases in most instances.[1]

There are many different ways to combine detailed industries to calculate an all-manufacturing average. In table 4 the average of weekly plant hours for 1976 under variant A reflects the use of production-worker employment weights. The figure for 1929 was calculated in a similar fashion and reflects employment weights for that year. This basis, with employment weights varying between the two years, yields a change of 23 percent.

If the focus is on capital inputs a more appropriate basis for combining plant hours in detailed industries is capital rather than employment. Both of the average weekly plant hours under variant B reflect the use of capital weights. Note that the level of each is substantially greater than the corresponding figures under variant A but that the change is somewhat smaller than the change calculated under A. Some of the detail underlying variant B may be seen in table 5. The 1976 average reflects the use of gross fixed assets (book value, from census) applied to average weekly plant hours at detailed (four-digit) industry levels to obtain two-digit averages and an average for all manufacturing. A similar procedure was used for 1929, except that horsepower was used to combine detailed industries in the

---

[1] Industry classifications were not the same in 1929 and in 1976. The two-digit industry comparisons in table 5 and the all-manufacturing results in table 4 reflect adjustments to bring about greater comparability at the two-digit level. See appendix F for fuller description.

TABLE 4
ALTERNATIVE MEASURES OF AVERAGE WEEKLY PLANT HOURS IN
MANUFACTURING AND THEIR CHANGE, 1929 TO 1976

Variant	1929	1976	Change (percent)
A[a]	66.5	81.8	23.0
B[b]	91.9	110.3	20.0
C[c]	—	—	24.7

[a] Hours for each detailed and major industry weighted by employment in each year.
[b] Capital weighted throughout. 1976: gross fixed assets at detailed (four-digit) level used to obtain average weekly plant hours for each major (two-digit) level and to obtain average weekly plant hours for all manufacturing. 1929: same as 1976 except that horsepower is used to combine detailed and major industry groups.
[c] Percentage change in capital-weighted average weekly plant hours for each major industry as shown in table 5 weighted by gross fixed capital stocks in 1972 prices for 1954 as estimated by Bureau of Labor Statistics.
SOURCE: Variant A, 1976, see table 1. All other statistics are estimates by author on the basis of data from Census Bureau.

absence of detailed statistics for gross fixed assets. The correlation between horsepower and gross fixed assets at a point of time is close.

Variant C makes use of average weekly plant hours for two-digit industries as calculated for variant B and as shown in table 5. The change for each two-digit industry from 1929 to 1976 was weighted by gross capital stocks in 1972 prices as estimated by the Bureau of Labor Statistics for 1954, which is roughly midway between 1929 and 1976. This variant, employing fixed weights, yields a change of 24.7 percent for all manufacturing. Variant C, which makes use of capital weights that are fixed (at the two-digit level), seems to be conceptually the most desirable measure, since a lengthening in weekly plant hours for all manufacturing should reflect a lengthening at the plant and detailed industry level and not merely a shift in mix toward industries that have always worked long plant hours. This study also used gross stock weights based on an average of the years 1951 through 1955 and similar weights reflecting the use of net stocks (after deduction of depreciation), but the changes from 1929 to 1976 all fell within a narrow range.

The 1929–1976 rise in average weekly plant hours occurred in the face of a substantial reduction in the average workweek of labor in manufacturing: The forty-hour week was the norm in 1976; in 1929 the workweek of labor was estimated by Kendrick on the basis

TABLE 5
AVERAGE WEEKLY PLANT HOURS AND THEIR CHANGE,
BY MAJOR INDUSTRY, 1929–1976

Industry	1929	1976	Change (percent)
Food	88.0	90.3	2.6
Tobacco	49.2	104.4	112.2
Textiles	66.8	115.6	73.0
Apparel	46.0	46.3	0.6
Lumber	58.2	62.6	7.6
Furniture	50.3	52.6	4.6
Paper	128.7	139.6	8.5
Printing and publishing	62.7	82.8	32.0
Chemicals	108.1	138.2	27.8
Petroleum	157.8	162.9	3.2
Rubber	103.7	120.0	15.7
Leather	49.4	45.6	−7.7
Stone, clay, and glass	104.6	119.3	14.1
Primary metals	125.5	142.4	13.5
Fabricated metals	55.6	77.8	39.9
Machinery	55.7	83.5	49.9
Electrical machinery	49.6	77.0	55.2
Transportation equipment	60.5	88.8	46.8
Instruments	59.5	76.6	28.7
Miscellaneous	49.3	62.1	26.0

SOURCE: Estimates by author based on data from Census Bureau. Reflects use of capital weights.

of census data at 50.4 measured by "prevailing" hours and 44.2 measured by actual hours.[2]

For all manufacturing combined, the 25 percent increase from 1929 to 1976 in average weekly plant hours may be compared with an increase of 166 percent in the real manufacturing capital stock (in 1972 prices) as estimated by the Bureau of Economic Analysis.[3] In

[2] John W. Kendrick, *Productivity Trends in the United States* (Princeton, N.J.: Princeton University Press for National Bureau of Economic Research, 1961). Albert Rees questioned Kendrick's estimate of actual hours for 1929 and offered an alternative estimate of 47.2 hours on the basis of a different analysis of the data. See Albert Rees, "New Measures of Wage-Earner Compensation in Manufacturing, 1914-57," National Bureau of Economic Research, Occasional Paper 75 (New York, 1960).

[3] John C. Musgrave, "Fixed Nonresidential Business and Residential Capital in the United States, 1925-75," *Survey of Current Business* vol. 56, no. 4 (April 1976), table 3.

terms of a compounded average annual rate of change, plant hours rose 0.47 percent per year, and the capital stock rose by 2.10 percent per year. The average annual rise in hours was thus 22 percent of the rise in stock.

The average weekly plant hours by two-digit industry shown in table 5 for 1929 and 1976 reflects the use of capital weights. As might be expected, industries that are largely continuous at the two-digit level—primary metals, paper, and petroleum—and industries in which shift work was common in 1929, such as rubber and stone (cement), show small changes in average weekly plant hours since 1929. Industries that have remained small scale, in the sense that single-plant companies still account for relatively large shares of total output, show either small increases or decreases and on balance are now operating fewer hours than in 1929; this decline has accompanied the decline in the average length of the workweek for labor. This pattern is prominent in apparel, leather, furniture, and lumber. Most other industries have experienced sizable increases in weekly hours worked by plants, food being an important exception. The increase is pronounced in the entire range of metal-fabricating industries (fabricated metals, machinery, transportation equipment, and instruments), where continuous operations are uncommon.

How Comparable Are 1929 and 1976? A direct comparison of 1976 with 1929 is valid if it can be assumed that the figures for both years were unaffected by seasonal influences and were at approximately the same position in the business cycle. Seasonal influences pose no problem for 1929, because data for that year refer to the year as a whole. They might be a problem for 1976, since the 1976 questionnaire (like all the recent Census Bureau surveys) refers to the fourth quarter rather than to the year as a whole. Implicit seasonal factors for two-digit manufacturing industries included in the Federal Reserve Board Index of Industrial Production were calculated for the fourth quarter of 1976. Since the mean was 99.7, it is reasonable to conclude that on average the fourth quarter is representative of the entire year.

The cyclical position of the two years is another matter. Even though manufacturing output peaked in the summer of 1929 and declined thereafter, the year as a whole was one of very high activity. In the recent period, by way of contrast, the economy generally and manufacturing production specifically were in the middle of recoveries that had started in the spring of 1975 after pronounced declines. Although manufacturing output in the fourth quarter of 1976 was within 1 percent of the peak reached in the third quarter of 1974, output was still well below rates of capacity utilization achieved in

TABLE 6

CAPACITY UTILIZATION IN MANUFACTURING: PEAK 1973 RATE AND FOURTH-QUARTER 1976 RATE

Measure of Capacity Utilization	1973		Fourth Quarter 1976	Percentage Difference 1973 over 1976
	Peak	Quarter		
Federal Reserve Board	87.8	3	80.6	8.9
Wharton	97.4	3	87.6	11.2
Bureau of Economic Analysis	86.0	1–2	81.0	6.2
Census	—	4 [a]	—	11.1

[a] Census surveys available only for fourth quarters.

SOURCES: Federal Reserve Board and Wharton—Council of Economic Advisers, *Economic Indicators;* Bureau of Economic Analysis, *Survey of Current Business;* and Bureau of the Census, *Survey of Plant Capacity* MQ-C.

the preceding expansion. A cyclical correction for 1976 based on relative utilization would be substantial. For example, using a 4 percent rate of unemployment as a basis for establishing the proper level of potential GNP, Denison concluded that his measure of output was 6.8 percent below potential in 1976 and 1.9 percent above potential in 1929.[4] If Denison's figures were applied to manufacturing to adjust for cyclical influences affecting each year, the change in weekly plant hours from 1929 to 1976 would have to be raised by an additional 8.9 percent $[(1.068/0.981) - 1]$.

The unemployment rate, of course, may not be the most appropriate guide for gauging relative utilization of plant capacity. Furthermore, Denison's figures apply essentially to the whole business economy; specific capacity utilization measures would seem more suitable for the purposes at hand. Table 6 shows for four measures of capacity utilization in manufacturing the peak rates reached in 1973, the rate in the fourth quarter of 1976 (seasonally adjusted where needed), and the percentage by which the former exceeded the latter. On the assumption that a 1973 peak is an appropriate high-level norm, these differences would provide the basis for an adjustment factor. The four differences average 9 percent. The average would be about 1 percent greater if based solely on measures of the Federal Reserve Board and the Wharton School, which make use of actual production in the calculation of relative utilization.

[4] Edward F. Denison, *Accounting for Slower Economic Growth* (Washington, D.C.: Brookings Institution, 1979), p. 13.

Other data from the census survey might provide the basis for calculating adjustment factors. In the current survey, the Census Bureau asks firms to report not only actual hours per day and days per week for plant operations but also similar data under preferred and practical capacity operations. In the fourth quarter of 1976, the average ratio of actual to preferred hours per week for two-digit industries was approximately 92 percent (table 7). This might constitute an adjustment factor if preferred capacity operations were taken as a norm.

TABLE 7

AVERAGE WEEKLY PLANT HOURS UNDER ACTUAL AND PREFERRED CAPACITY OPERATIONS, FOURTH QUARTER 1976

Industry	Actual	Preferred	Ratio of Actual to Preferred
Food	74.9	84.8	88.3
Tobacco	91.0	91.0	100.0
Textiles	110.2	122.1	90.2
Apparel	42.5	45.9	92.6
Lumber	58.1	64.8	89.7
Furniture	51.0	60.2	84.7
Paper	114.6	125.7	91.2
Printing and publishing	82.3	89.6	91.8
Chemicals	112.2	117.0	95.9
Petroleum	140.0	143.9	97.3
Rubber	108.0	116.0	93.1
Leather	44.5	48.4	91.9
Stone, clay, and glass	97.5	104.4	93.4
Primary metals	118.6	132.4	89.6
Fabricated metals	74.9	84.8	88.3
Machinery	79.6	87.4	91.1
Electrical machinery	73.4	84.8	86.6
Transportation equipment	87.4	89.4	97.8
Instruments	68.6	77.5	88.5
Miscellaneous	57.1	64.8	88.1
Average based on employment weights	—	—	91.5
Average based on gross fixed assets weights	—	—	91.8

SOURCE: Basic data for the first two columns: Bureau of the Census. See table 8 for source of gross fixed assets weights.

TABLE 8

ACTUAL WEEKLY PLANT HOURS AS PERCENTAGE OF WEEKLY PLANT HOURS
AT PREFERRED RATES OF CAPACITY UTILIZATION, BY INDUSTRY,
FOURTH QUARTER 1973 AND FOURTH QUARTER 1976

Industry	1973	1976	Ratio of 1976 to 1973
Food	90.5	88.3	97.6
Tobacco	94.5	100.0	105.8
Textiles	93.4	90.2	96.6
Lumber	95.2	89.7	94.2
Furniture	92.7	84.7	91.4
Paper	93.0	91.2	98.1
Chemicals	94.1	95.9	101.9
Petroleum	99.5	97.3	97.8
Rubber	93.4	93.1	99.7
Stone, clay, and glass	97.2	93.4	96.1
Primary metals	98.1	89.6	91.3
Fabricated metals	96.1	88.3	91.9
Machinery	101.9	91.1	89.4
Electrical machinery	96.9	86.6	89.4
Transportation equipment	98.9	97.8	98.9
Instruments	96.2	88.5	92.0
Total manufacturing[a]	—	—	95.7

[a] Weighted by 1974 gross fixed assets in 1972 dollars as estimated by the Bureau of Labor Statistics and based on industries shown.

SOURCE: Based on unpublished census data; gross fixed assets weights from Bureau of Labor Statistics, *Capital Stock Estimates for Input-Output Industries: Methods and Data*, Bulletin 2034, 1979.

The difficulty with capacity utilization measures is that they refer to output, but weekly plant hours are an aspect of input. Output may fall below capacity not because shifts are reduced but because operations are reduced below normal through layoffs. Suppose a direct comparison were made of weekly plant hours in 1976 and 1973. If weights are held constant in both years, the change in average weekly plant hours from the fourth quarter of 1973 to the fourth quarter of 1976 ranges from about ½ of 1 percent to 1½ percent, depending on whether fixed capital or employment is used for weighting. If the 1973–1976 experience is typical, it suggests that, between the top of the boom and midway in a recovery, cyclical variations in the number of shifts worked per day and in the number of days worked per week in the aggregate are not very great.

I believe that a direct comparison of plant hours gives too small an adjustment, whereas a comparison of capacity utilization rates gives too large an adjustment. A compromise might involve calculating first the ratio of actual to preferred average weekly plant hours in 1973 and 1976 and then the 1976 figure as a percent of the 1973 figure. This is done in table 8, which shows that in most industries the 1976 ratios are below those of 1973. Using gross fixed assets to weight the differences yields an average decline of 4.3 percent for all industries combined.

Figures for 1929 like those for 1976 are not available. Economists at the Brookings Institution[5] estimated manufacturing capacity utilization in 1929 to be 83 percent of practical capacity, but there is no reason to believe that the definitions used then are the same as those embodied in the Census Bureau surveys. One might approximate an adjustment for 1929 by fitting a trend line through indexes of production for census years from, say, 1899 to 1929 and noting the deviation from trend in 1929. Although on this basis output in 1929 appears somewhat high, this study makes no adjustment for 1929, mainly because of data limitations. This leaves a 4.5 percent figure $[(1 \div 0.957) - 1]$ with which to adjust the changes in weekly plant hours shown in table 4.

Changes in Capital Stocks and Capital-Output Ratios

One reason for undertaking this study was to determine how capital-output ratios are affected when the change in plant hours is taken into account. Without taking account of plant hours, investigators such as Creamer and Kendrick found widespread declines among industries and a strong decline overall for the period being investigated here.[6]

Table 9 shows for two-digit industries average annual rates of change from 1929 to 1976 in weekly plant hours, in fixed capital before and after an adjustment for changes in weekly plant hours, and ratios of the change in plant hours to the change in fixed capital. No further adjustment has been made in this particular table for differences in the stage of business cycle between the two years. The changes in capital stock before adjustment for plant hours are

---

[5] Edward G. Nourse and Associates, *America's Capacity to Produce* (Washington, D.C.: Brookings Institution, 1934), p. 307.

[6] Daniel Creamer, Sergei Dobrovolsky, and Israel Borenstein, *Capital in Manufacturing and Mining: Its Formation and Financing* (Princeton, N.J.: Princeton University Press for National Bureau of Economic Research, 1960). See also John W. Kendrick, *Productivity Trends in the United States* (Princeton, N.J.: Princeton University Press for National Bureau of Economic Research, 1961).

TABLE 9

AVERAGE ANNUAL RATE OF CHANGE IN WEEKLY PLANT HOURS,
FIXED CAPITAL, AND FIXED CAPITAL ADJUSTED BY PLANT HOURS, AND
RATIO OF CHANGE IN PLANT HOURS TO CHANGE IN FIXED CAPITAL,
1929 TO 1976

| | Average Annual Rate of Change | | | |
Industry	Weekly plant hours	Fixed capital	Fixed capital adjusted by plant hours	Change in Plant Hours/ Change in Fixed Capital[a]
Food	0.06	0.19	0.25	0.28
Tobacco	1.61	2.42	4.08	0.66
Textiles	1.17	1.37	2.56	0.86
Apparel	0.01	0.98	1.00	0.01
Lumber	0.16	−0.92	−0.76	—
Furniture	0.10	0.38	0.48	0.25
Paper	0.17	1.92	2.09	0.09
Printing and publishing	0.59	1.39	1.98	0.42
Chemicals	0.52	3.66	4.21	0.14
Petroleum	0.07	2.92	2.99	0.02
Rubber	0.31	2.36	2.68	0.13
Leather	−0.17	−1.07	−1.24	0.16
Stone, clay, and glass	0.28	1.05	1.34	0.26
Primary metals	0.27	2.13	2.40	0.13
Fabricated metals	0.72	3.53	4.28	0.20
Machinery	0.86	3.32	4.21	0.26
Electrical machinery	0.94	4.16	5.14	0.23
Transportation equipment	0.82	2.68	3.52	0.31
Instruments	0.54	3.53	4.09	0.15
Miscellaneous	0.49	0.92	1.42	0.53

[a] Based on unrounded data.

SOURCES: Table 4; Creamer, Dobrovolsky, and Borenstein, *Capital in Manufacturing and Mining*, table A-9, for 1929-1948; and John W. Kendrick and Elliott S. Grossman, *Productivity in the United States: Trends and Cycles* (Baltimore, Md.: John Hopkins University Press, 1980), for 1948-1976.

Creamer's estimates of changes in net stocks (gross stocks less depreciation) from 1929 to 1948, linked to Kendrick's estimates of changes in gross stocks from 1948 to 1976. It would obviously be preferable if industry changes over the entire forty-seven-year span could be calculated on a completely consistent basis—gross or net—but this information is not available. It may be of some importance that, according to estimates of the Bureau of Economic Analysis, fixed capital stocks in manufacturing measured in 1972 prices increased by 19.1 percent on a gross basis and by 19.7 percent on a net basis from 1929 to 1948.[7]

It is not the intention of this study to discuss at length the relative merits of gross as compared to net stocks in measuring fixed capital input. There is general agreement that what is wanted in a measure of fixed capital input is the ability of capital to contribute to production, but there has been disagreement about how this is best measured. In addition, the gaps in the data for early periods have been serious. Denison has adopted a stock figure that gives a weight of ¾ to gross stocks and ¼ to corresponding net stocks.[8] Creamer used net stocks, because net figures were the only ones available. Kendrick, following Creamer, employed net stocks in his earlier studies but shifted to a fully gross measure in his latest estimates.

In support of his position, Denison has noted that if all capital goods were of the "wonderful one-hoss shay" variety, a gross measure would be appropriate, because the services of the capital good would remain undiminished throughout its life. This is an extreme assumption, even though using it does not lead to much error in practice. Some capital goods do provide fewer services as they age, unless they are kept up through rising maintenance and repair expenditures, which are a deduction from net output. Denison has also noted that, where different vintages of a capital good exist, the older good is likely to be used less fully.[9]

In almost all industries, the change in average weekly plant hours from 1929 to 1976 has reinforced the corresponding change in the fixed capital stock without regard to hours. Below is a frequency distribution of the average annual rate of change in weekly plant hours as a percentage of the average annual rate of change in stocks for twenty industries (from last column of table 9).

[7] John Musgrave, "Fixed Nonresidential Business and Residential Capital in the United States, 1925-75," *Survey of Current Business*, vol. 56, no. 4 (April 1976), pp. 46-52.

[8] Edward F. Denison, *Accounting for U.S. Economic Growth 1929-1969* (Washington, D.C.: Brookings Institution, 1974), p. 55.

[9] Edward F. Denison, *Why Growth Rates Differ* (Washington, D.C.: Brookings Institution, 1967), pp. 140-41.

	Number of Industries
Offsetting	1
Change in plant hours	
and in stocks, both positive:	18
Ratio	
Up to 9.9 percent	3
10 to 19.9 percent	4
20 to 29.9 percent	6
30 percent and over	5
Change in plant hours and	
in stocks, both negative	1
Total	20

In the lumber industry, a decline in stocks was partly offset by a rise in weekly plant hours, and in the leather industry the decline in hours reinforced the decline in stocks. Otherwise the signs of change in plant hours and stocks are positive, eleven of twenty industries having ratios of 20 percent or more. The seven industries with ratios of less than 20 percent include apparel, in which plant hours were virtually unchanged from 1929 to 1976, and the paper, chemicals, rubber, and petroleum industries, in which either continuous operations or very long weekly plant hours have been the rule for a long time.

How would changes in capital-output ratios be altered by taking account of the change in average weekly plant hours? Table 10 shows indexes of output and capital-output ratios for two-digit industries before and after an adjustment for changes in weekly plant hours. From 1929 to 1976, capital-output ratios before adjustment declined in all industries; after adjustment, tobacco and machinery showed rising ratios, and two industries—textiles and printing—showed little change. Before adjustment for the rise in the length of the plant workweek, the (gross) capital-output ratio for all manufacturing declined by 45 percent, but after adjustment the decrease was 31 percent (table 11).

Estimates of average weekly plant hours do not exist for any interim years but are being prepared. Suppose the change in average weekly plant hours over the entire period is assumed to have been steady and continuous, so that the change over any intervening period was proportional to the number of years since 1929. Then an estimate for the change in average weekly plant hours from 1929 to 1948 is obtained by taking 19/47 of the 1929–1976 change. There is reason to believe that changes were concentrated in the early post–World War II years, but a consideration of these issues is best left to a later time.

TABLE 10

1976 INDEXES OF OUTPUT AND CAPITAL-OUTPUT RATIOS BEFORE AND AFTER ADJUSTMENT FOR CHANGES IN AVERAGE WEEKLY PLANT HOURS
(1929 = 100)

Industry	Index of Output	Capital-Output Ratios	
		Before hours adjustment	After hours adjustment
Food	361	30	31
Tobacco	374	82	175
Textiles	342	56	96
Apparel	348	46	46
Lumber	210	31	34
Furniture	329	36	38
Paper	570	43	46
Printing and publishing	322	59	78
Chemicals	1501	36	46
Petroleum	535	72	74
Rubber	655	46	53
Leather	114	53	49
Stone, clay, and glass	354	46	53
Primary metals	192	141	176
Fabricated metals	420	122	170
Machinery	511	91	136
Electrical machinery	1370	50	77
Transportation equipment	576	60	88
Instruments	974	52	67
Miscellaneous	490	31	40

SOURCES: Capital-output ratios calculated by the author from data in the following sources. Output data: for 1929-1948, Kendrick, *Productivity Trends;* for 1948-1976, Bureau of Economic Analysis, *The National Income and Product Accounts of the United States, 1929-74, Statistical Tables*, p. 184, and *Survey of Current Business,* July 1979, p. 52. Fixed capital data: for 1929-1948, Creamer, Dobrovolsky, and Borenstein, *Capital in Manufacturing and Mining,* and for 1948-1976, Kendrick and Grossman, *Productivity in the United States.* The source for data on plant hours is table 5 of this volume.

For all manufacturing combined, the 19 percent rise in gross stocks from 1929 to 1948 was only slightly larger than the 14.7 percent rise in average weekly plant hours that occurred if the change in hours from 1929 to 1976 was steady and continuous. Omitting the change in average weekly plant hours probably means a serious understatement of the change in capital input for this early postwar period. Longer plant hours must have been an important factor in

TABLE 11

1976 INDEXES OF MANUFACTURING OUTPUT, FIXED CAPITAL, AND CAPITAL-OUTPUT RATIOS, WITH AND WITHOUT ADJUSTMENT FOR CHANGES IN AVERAGE WEEKLY PLANT HOURS
(1929 = 100)

	Index
Output	480.8
Fixed capital—gross	265.9
Fixed capital—net	254.7
Fixed capital with hours adjustment	
Gross[a]	331.6
Net[b]	317.6
Capital-output ratios	
Gross	
Without hours adjustment	55.3
With hours adjustment	69.0
Net	
Without hours adjustment	53.0
With hours adjustment	66.0

[a] Index of gross fixed capital times 124.7.
[b] Index of net fixed capital times 124.7.
SOURCES: See table 10 for sources of output data and plant hours. Fixed capital is from Bureau of Economic Analysis, *Survey of Current Business:* 1929 data are from the August 1976 issue, p. 48; 1976 data are from the August 1979 issue, part II, p. 62.

the growth of conventionally measured productivity in this period. Fellner had called attention to abnormally low capital-output ratios during the war.[10] In his 1957 article Solow speculated that a secular increase in shift work would explain at least part of the 1943–1949 deviations from his long-run relationship between output and capital.[11]

Changes in Total Factor Productivity

When the change in capital input is measured solely by the change in the stock of capital, as is now done by investigators such as Denison and Kendrick, any increased output attributable to the lengthening in capital hours should be included in the increase in total factor pro-

[10] See William Fellner, *Trends and Cycles in Economic Activity* (New York: Henry Holt, 1956), p. 92.
[11] See Robert Solow, "Technical Change and the Aggregate Production Function," *Review of Economics and Statistics* (August 1957), pp. 312-20.

ductivity. To what extent is the growth in total factor productivity from 1929 to 1976 a reflection of the lengthening of average weekly plant hours?

The economic influences underlying the growth of total factor productivity for the whole economy or for an important industry division such as manufacturing are not easy to pin down. John Kendrick and Nestor Terleckyj investigated a large number of influences in the manufacturing sector for selected periods from 1899 to 1966.[12] For the 1899–1952 period, Terleckyj found only three explanatory variables that were significantly related to rates of change in total factor productivity by industry: the rate of change of output, the amplitude of fluctuation of output, and the ratio of research and development outlays to sales. In a similar vein, Kendrick found for the 1948–1966 period only the last two variables to be significantly related to industry rates of change in total factor productivity. Table 12, taken directly from Kendrick, gives a matrix of his correlation results. The highest correlation coefficient in column 1 is for the rate of change in output. As Kendrick notes, however, this is not really satisfactory as an explanatory variable, because it is not clear whether it is the cause or the result of the rise in total factor productivity.[13]

Kendrick and Grossman have recently revised and updated Kendrick's time series on total factor productivity by industry from 1948 to 1976.[14] These estimates can be linked to Kendrick's estimates for the 1929–1948 period to yield changes from 1929 to 1976. A simple correlation based on twenty industries yields a correlation coefficient of 0.45, which is significant at the .05 level. A high correlation coefficient should not be expected, since there are probably many influences associated with the growth of total factor productivity in each industry, and a comprehensive study of all the factors influencing the growth of productivity is beyond the scope of this particular study. Nonetheless, these are important results, since they demonstrate for the first time a link between the growth of total factor productivity and the change in the length of the plant workweek at the two-digit industry level.

---

[12] John W. Kendrick, *Postwar Productivity Trends in the United States, 1948-1969* (New York: Columbia University Press for National Bureau of Economic Research, 1973), pp. 132-43; Nestor Terleckyj, "Factors Underlying Productivity: Some Empirical Observations," *Journal of the American Statistical Association* (June 1958), p. 593, and "Sources of Productivity Change: A Pilot Study Based on the Experience of American Manufacturing Industries, 1948-1953" (Ph.D. diss., Columbia University, 1959).

[13] Kendrick, *Postwar Productivity Trends*, p. 141.

[14] Kendrick and Grossman, *Productivity in the United States.*

TABLE 12

MATRIX OF SIMPLE CORRELATION COEFFICIENTS, RATES OF CHANGE IN TOTAL
FACTOR PRODUCTIVITY VERSUS NINE INDEPENDENT VARIABLES,
FOR TWENTY-ONE U.S. MANUFACTURING INDUSTRY GROUPS, 1948–1966

	(1)	(2)	(3)	(4)	(5)	(6)	(7)	(8)	(9)	(10)
1. Rate of change in productivity	1.000	0.649[a]	0.248	0.106	0.397	0.397	0.327	0.044	0.112	−0.387
2. Rate of change in output	0.649[a]	1.000	0.801[a]	0.341	0.745[a]	0.762[a]	0.430	0.513[b]	−0.237	0.050
3. Rate of change in real capital	0.248	0.801[a]	1.000	0.311	0.633[a]	0.777[a]	0.270	0.541[b]	−0.075	0.229
4. Variability of output changes	0.106	0.341	0.311	1.000	0.201	0.431	0.125	0.372	0.133	0.249
5. Average education per employee	0.397	0.745[a]	0.633[a]	0.201	1.000	0.571[a]	0.437[b]	0.315	−0.413	0.124
6. Ratio of R&D[c] to sales	0.397	0.762[a]	0.777[a]	0.431	0.571[a]	1.000	0.282	0.510[b]	−0.004	−0.100
7. Average hours worked	0.327	0.430	0.270	0.125	0.437[b]	0.282	1.000	0.292	−0.188	0.103
8. Concentration ratio	0.044	0.513[b]	0.541[b]	0.372	0.315	0.510[b]	0.292	1.000	−0.264	0.425
9. Rate of change in concentration	0.112	−0.237	−0.075	0.133	−0.413	−0.004	−0.188	−0.264	1.000	−0.350
10. Unionization ratio	−0.387	0.050	0.229	0.249	0.124	−0.100	0.103	0.425	−0.350	1.000

[a] Significant at .01 level.
[b] Significant at .05 level.
[c] Research and development.

SOURCE: Kendrick, *Postwar Productivity Trends*, table 6-12.

Estimates of average weekly plant hours for 1948 are not now available, but the simple assumption can be made that the change in average hours from 1929 to 1948 was 19/47 of the 1929–1976 change. Even with crude estimates such as these, we should expect that the correlation between changes in total factor productivity and in weekly plant hours by industry was greater from 1929 to 1948 than from 1929 to 1976. This is because the "deficits" in the capital stock caused by low investment during the depression and World War II were still severe in 1948 and had to be made up by longer weekly plant hours. For the shorter period the correlation coefficient of 0.52 is somewhat higher than it is for the full forty-seven-year span.

Some Further Aspects of the Change in Weekly Plant Hours

This chapter concludes with a presentation of some additional characteristics of the 1929 data and a comparison with the present. Plant size, regional patterns, and continuous industries are discussed.

Size. In the tables that follow, size is measured by value added per establishment and is presented for four value-added class intervals. Value added is a better measure of size than employment or fixed assets, insofar as labor and capital are substitutes. To the extent that large plants (measured by value added) also tend to use more capital-intensive methods than average, however, the interpretation of size presented here is not free of ambiguity.

Summary figures for 1929 (table 13) suggest a positive relationship between number of shifts per day, plant hours per day, and plant hours per week, on the one hand, and plant size, on the other. The relationship is not strong, however; the positive relationship (omitting the smallest size class, for which samples are thin) does not hold for eight of fourteen major industries. For 1976 the positive relationship is much stronger. If the smallest class interval is excluded, the positive relationship shows up in every two-digit industry, including such industries as apparel, lumber, furniture, and leather, in which most plants operate a single shift. Moreover, the elasticity of plant hours with respect to size is greater than in 1929. In 1976, weekly hours for the largest size class were more than double those for the smallest class whereas in 1929 weekly hours in the largest size class were only 28 percent greater than those in the bottom group.

Regions. Table 14 provides information on the prevalence of late-shift work in four census regions. Industry detail for both years is given in appendix G. Table 14 shows the proportions of total wage earner

TABLE 13

Average Plant Operations by Value-Added Class, 1929 and 1976

	Less than $100,000	$100,000 to $999,999	$1,000,000 to $4,999,999	$5,000,000 and Over
1929				
Average number of shifts	1.2	1.2	1.4	1.5
Average hours per day	10.3	11.0	12.5	12.9
Average days per week	5.7	5.7	5.8	5.9
Average hours per week	58.9	62.7	72.9	75.7
1976				
Average number of shifts	1.1	1.2	1.7	2.2
Average hours per day	9.2	10.2	13.6	18.2
Average days per week	5.1	5.1	5.2	5.5
Average hours per week	47.1	51.5	69.8	100.0

Source: U.S. Department of Commerce, Bureau of the Census, unpublished data.

employment in plants operating fewer than 2 shifts, 2 to 2.9 shifts, and 3 or more shifts for all industries. For manufacturing as a whole plants operating two or more shifts in 1929 were most prevalent in the South and West and least prevalent in the Northeast; in fact, the prevalence in the South was more than 60 percent greater than in the Northeast. The proportion with 2 or more shifts was highest in the South for about half the major industries. By 1976, however, the regional patterns had changed considerably. For manufacturing as a whole, all regions showed increased proportions of multiple-shift plants, but the North-central region was highest; as in 1929, the Northeast was lowest. The spread between the lowest and highest proportion of plants operating 2 or more shifts was considerably diminished—less than 25 percent for all manufacturing. This reduction in dispersion was also evident for major industries. In each industry the relative dispersion—measured by the range of regional percentages relative to the industry mean—was much lower in 1976 than in 1929.

On the surface it would appear that half a century ago plants in the South and West operated the longest weekly hours, possibly because manufacturing was in its early stages of development in these regions and capital was relatively scarce. By 1976 these regional differences were greatly reduced, perhaps because capital was readily available in all parts of the nation and what had been the best

TABLE 14

DISTRIBUTION OF EMPLOYMENT IN MANUFACTURING BY NUMBER
OF SHIFTS OPERATED PER PLANT AND BY REGION, 1929 AND 1976
(percent)

Region	Fewer Than 2 Shifts	2 to 2.9 Shifts	3 or More Shifts	2 or More Shifts
1929				
Northeast	82	10	8	18
North-central	79	10	11	21
South	71	19	10	29
West	75	15	11	25
1976				
Northeast	50	25	26	50
North-central	38	34	28	62
South	45	21	34	55
West	48	28	24	52

NOTE: 1929 figures exclude railroad repair shops.
SOURCE: Unpublished data from Bureau of the Census.

practice before was now the standard in all regions. The extent of union organization may also have been a factor, but these are only speculations that are not discussed further in this study.

Continuous Industries. Continuous operations are fairly common in American manufacturing today, representing technological trends that have been going on for some time. The term "continuous" tends to be used somewhat loosely in industry literature. Sometimes it refers to industries such as petroleum refining or industrial chemicals, in which inputs are transformed into outputs through an uninterrupted production process or combination of processes. The key to the term "continuous" is the prohibitive marginal costs of interruption at, say, the end of a day.[15] Blast furnaces operations are continuous, because a blast furnace cannot be economically shut down at the end of a day and relit the following morning. One also sees references, however, to "continuous hot strip mills." The hot rolling of (sheet and) strip is one stage in steel manufacture, which may involve interruption at the beginning or the end of the operation. It is "continuous" in com-

---

[15] See Gordon C. Winston, "The Theory of Capital Utilization and Idleness," *Journal of Economic Literature*, vol. 12, no. 4 (December 1974), pp. 1301-20.

parison to the older method, which involved a considerable amount of hand work. Continuous operations such as those found in petroleum refining stand in contrast to batch operations, in which goods are processed through a series of discrete steps, at the end of any of which production could be halted at comparatively little incremental cost. Continuous processes are usually characterized by a substitution of capital for labor and frequently by operation of the capital around the clock. A rise in the capital-labor ratio and a reduction of the time during which fixed capital is idle are probably the two main results of the trend toward continuous processes.

At the two-digit level, a few industries—paper, chemicals, petroleum, and primary metals—are commonly thought of as constituting the continuous segment of American manufacturing. These four accounted for 41.4 percent of the gross fixed assets reported to the Census Bureau by all manufacturing establishments at the end of 1976. However, many four-digit industries within these two-digit industries work a much shorter week. If continuous industries are defined as those in which *all* plants work 168 hours a week, the proportion is greatly reduced.

Industries with *some* continuous technology would stand at the opposite extreme from those in which every plant worked 168 hours. In response to a special request, the Census Bureau found 111 four-digit industries of approximately 450 in which at least one plant reported operating 168 hours per week in the fourth quarter of 1976. These 111 industries, including their noncontinuous portions, accounted for 35 percent of employment and 54 percent of gross fixed assets in the fourth quarter of 1976 (table 15).[16]

Several factors explain why the same four-digit industry may simultaneously embrace plants working 168 hours and plants working less than 168 hours per week. A plant workweek of 168 hours might be a temporary response to some unusual demand. Second, many four-digit industries are broad in their scope and embrace plants producing quite different commodities. Industry 3321, blast furnaces and steel mills, embraces blast furnace and raw steel plants, which operate continuously through the week, as well as rolling mills, which may or may not operate around the clock. Third, different processes for an identical product may be involved. Finally, the 168-hour plant may represent a completely new technology that has just been introduced.

The Georgia-Pacific Company publishes annual capacity data for each of its plants and the number of shifts underlying the capacity

---

16 U.S. Department of Commerce, Bureau of the Census, unpublished data.

TABLE 15

INDUSTRIES IN WHICH AT LEAST ONE ESTABLISHMENT OPERATED 168 HOURS PER WEEK IN THE FOURTH QUARTER OF 1976

2022	2261	2812	2895	3313	3511
2023	2262	2813	2899	3315	3519
2026	2272	2816	2911	3316	3532
2033	2282	2819	2952	3331	3545
2034	2296	2821	3069	3332	3563
2046	2436	2822	3079	3333	3624
2051	2499	2823	3211	3334	3634
2063	2611	2824	3221	3339	3644
2075	2621	2833	3229	3341	3652
2079	2631	2834	3241	3353	3662
2082	2643	2843	3251	3357	3714
2084	2647	2844	3253	3411	3728
2095	2654	2861	3263	3429	3731
2099	2661	2865	3269	3443	3761
2221	2711	2869	3275	3465	3795
2241	2732	2873	3295	3483	3799
2253	2751	2874	3296	3489	3841
2257	2752	2879	3312	3498	3861

NOTE: Three industries are not shown in order to avoid disclosure. The meaning of SIC numbers is explained in the Census of Manufactures.

SOURCE: Bureau of the Census, unpublished data.

calculations. Table 16 illustrates data for certain commodities in which continuous and noncontinuous plants exist simultaneously in the United States.

Table 17 presents some data on the trend in the importance of continuous industries, a continuous industry being defined as one having at least one plant operating 168 hours a week. This particular comparison is based on 120 industries or industry groups that were judged comparable in 1929 and 1976.

The census surveys do not reveal how respondents in plants that typically operate without interruption reported actual allowance for downtime, that is, time out for repairs and maintenance under actual operations. Some industries commonly thought of as operating without interruption through the day reported that they operated less than twenty-four hours a day. Such a figure could be correct only if based on the experience of an extended period, such as a year. The assumption is made in this study that some plants that might otherwise report they operated 168 hours per week had reported to the Census Bureau

TABLE 16

ANNUAL CAPACITIES FOR SELECTED ITEMS
MADE BY GEORGIA-PACIFIC COMPANY

Product and Type of Operation	Annual Capacity
Panelboard coating and vinyl overlay	
Continuous (print overlay)	150.0 million square feet
2-shift 5-day (vinyl overlay)	64.5 million square feet
3-shift 5-day (paper coating)	112.0 million square feet
Gypsum wallboard	
Continuous	2,123.0 million square feet
3-shift 5-day	119.0 million square feet
Tissue paper products	
Continuous	5.3 million cases
3-shift 5-day	8.2 million cases
2-shift 6-day	1.6 million cases
Grocery bags	
Continuous	42,000 tons
3-shift 5-day	53,000 tons

SOURCE: Georgia-Pacific, *1976 Annual Report.*

a figure that was as much as 10 percent less than 168 hours—a reasonable but arbitrary figure—for downtime. Consequently it was decided that any industry with an average of 150 hours per week or more could be considered continuous.[17] The paragraphs below present some estimates showing how such industries have changed over time.

Within each four-digit industry in 1976, it was possible to obtain unpublished Census Bureau tabulations of plants working 150 hours or more per week and their share of industry employment. Data showing shares of gross fixed assets would have been preferable but were not available. In any case the percentages for each four-digit industry were weighted by 1976 gross fixed assets to obtain a percentage for each two-digit industry; combining these percentages for each two-digit industry with gross fixed assets weights yields a figure for all manufacturing. For 1976 this is the 27.9 percent given at the top of table 18. Similar calculations for 1929 based on employment shares at the most detailed level, but using horsepower to combine industries,

---

[17] A plant may work continuously through the week but not necessarily through the year. Plants processing seasonal commodities may fall into this category. The 1929 schedule called for days operated per year, but this information, though desirable, has not been requested in the current surveys.

TABLE 17

Trend in Number of Continuous Manufacturing Industries, 1929 to 1976

	Number of Industries
No plant operating 168 hours per week in either 1929 or 1976	80
At least one continuous plant in 1976 and none in 1929	20
At least one continuous plant in 1929 and none in 1976	4
At least one continuous plant in 1929 and in 1976	16
Total	120

NOTE: In this table "continuous industry" is defined as one having at least one plant that operated 168 hours per week. This particular comparison is limited to industries judged comparable with respect to types of products produced from 1929 to 1976.

SOURCE: Author, based on unpublished census data.

yielded a figure of 16.0 percent. Each percentage would be a little higher if industry classifications were adjusted for conformity with one another as in table 5.

The second line of table 18 embodies two adjustments, in the first of which two-digit industries are adjusted for conformity as in table 5. Then, to obtain a figure for all manufacturing in each year, two-digit industries are combined with a single set of weights: Bureau of Labor Statistics gross stocks in 1972 prices for the years 1951–1955. The variant with constant weights yields a smaller percentage change in the continuous proportions from 1929 to 1976 than the other variant. The data suggest a shift in mix in the manufacturing stock of fixed capital—at the two-digit level—toward continuousness from 1929 to 1976, as well as shifts within industries.

TABLE 18

Alternative Measures of Proportion of Manufacturing Fixed Capital Operated Continuously, 1929 and 1976

Variant	1929	1976
A[a]	16.0	27.9
B[b]	20.0	28.0

NOTE: *Continuously* refers to plants operating 150 hours per week or more.

[a] As industry classifications existed in each year.

[b] Comparable industry classifications at two-digit level.

3

Reasons for Changes in Average
Weekly Plant Hours
from 1929 to 1976

This chapter is a statistical analysis of factors that account for the change in average weekly plant hours from 1929 to 1976. Using the detailed industry as the unit of observation, the analysis focuses on long-run rather than cyclical influences. The chapter begins with a discussion of the theory of shift work. The theory that has developed applies to the individual firm under static conditions, but it has applicability to long-run changes. Partly on the basis of the theory, this study analyzes variations in average weekly plant hours by industry in 1976 and 1929 and then takes up industry changes over time.

Theory of Shift Work

Our understanding of shift work has been enhanced since the appearance of Marris's important work in 1964.[1] In recent years the names of Winston and of Betancourt and Clague have been prominent.[2] Marris stressed that the individual businessman, when considering a new investment, must make a decision regarding the use of his fixed capital under what he expects to be his normal operating conditions. At any given time normal conditions may not prevail, since fluctuations in demand may cause firms to alter their plant hours by adding or dropping shifts. But these are cyclical rather than long-run considerations.

When a business contemplates building a new factory and is faced with a decision regarding capital requirements, it can plan to use a

---

[1] Robin Marris, *The Economics of Capital Utilization* (Cambridge: Cambridge University Press, 1964).

[2] See, for example, Gordon C. Winston, "Capital Utilization in Economic Development," *Economic Journal*, vol. 81, no. 321 (March 1971), pp. 36-60; and Roger R. Betancourt and Christopher K. Clague, "An Economic Analysis of Capital Utilization," *Southern Economic Journal*, vol. 42, no. 1 (July 1975), pp. 69-78. Fuller listings appear in the bibliography.

given stock of capital intensively (say, two shifts) or a larger stock less intensively (say, one shift). The decision regarding shifts is no less an aspect of the firm's capital requirements than is the size of the stock itself. Shifts and changes in shifts are a dimension of capital and cannot be ignored in analyzing the growth of capital and the growth of output over time. The traditional approach of measuring capital input by capital available or in place must be extended to include the number of shifts or weekly hours that the capital is available.

The use of multiple shifts is a form of economizing in the use of capital and of reducing capital costs per unit of output. The more capital-intensive the production process, the greater the incentive to use multiple shifts. Firms do not push utilization to some kind of maximum (say, twenty-four hours per day), however, because they encounter rising marginal costs of various kinds, of which labor is ordinarily the most important. Premium pay is usually required for second and third shifts because workers dislike working other than conventional daytime hours. Also employers may conceivably be unwilling to use late shifts because labor productivity may be poorer on second and third than on first shifts. But other variable costs besides labor may be involved. Winston stresses that some variable inputs show daily rhythms in their prices, and to this extent firms will choose to produce when such costs are lowest rather than when they are at a peak. In addition, capital costs may rise, since late-shift work will involve greater maintenance expense and user-cost depreciation. In terms of planned operations, the optimal number of shifts is reached when the net saving in capital costs per unit is just offset by the added variable costs associated with shift work.

As the earlier tabulations suggest, shift work tends to be found in larger plants, but this does not reflect a pure size effect. Indeed, Marris maintained that when the individual firm is faced with a situation where output is given, size of plant is inversely related to shift work, because by opting for a smaller plant with intensive utilization rather than a larger plant with less intensive utilization, the firm loses the advantages of some economies of scale.[3] Betancourt and Clague in their study of French and Japanese plants found that plant size was not a significant influence on shift work after allowance was made for the inverse effect noted above.[4] The refined cost data required to investigate such an influence were not available. This

---

[3] Marris, *The Economics of Capital Utilization*, pp. 80-92.

[4] Roger R. Betancourt and Christopher K. Clague, "An Econometric Analysis of Capital Utilization," *International Economic Review*, vol. 19, no. 1 (February 1978), p. 219.

study, however, did investigate the possibility that size may be important in limiting the use of shift work where scale is very small, as Marris has suggested. In the same vein, proprietors who are considering the use of extra shifts but are unwilling to delegate managerial responsibilities to late-shift supervisors may find their plant operations limited to a single shift, or a single shift with some overtime, because they value their leisure highly. Two other influences that Winston and Betancourt and Clague stress in their microanalysis are relative factor prices and the elasticity of substitution, or the ease with which labor and capital may be substituted for one another in response to changing relative factor prices. Shift work is encouraged when capital prices are high relative to those of labor, but for this investigation there was no way of differentiating capital prices among detailed industries. Finally, the greater the elasticity of substitution, the greater the use of shift work. Even though these are interesting and important theoretical issues, data problems were judged too severe for their implementation in this particular study.

The theoretical principles of shift work outlined are static principles applicable to the plant or firm, but it is necessary to explain changes in shift work by industry over almost half a century during which technology, markets, factor supplies, relative prices, and the institutional and legal settings have changed. We still lack an appropriate theoretical model, which would combine the static principles at the micro level with the theory of growth at the macro level.[5] No such model will be found here. Despite the many difficulties, I believe that some insights can be gained through the statistical analysis described below, recognizing that what is attempted is only a start.

Specific Influences Investigated

The pages that follow discuss specific influences that were investigated statistically. Some of the independent variables chosen are those suggested by the microtheory, whereas others are suggested by some broad facts we know about the economy. Measuring certain variables suggested by theory and rejecting others reflect judgments concerning the adequacy of the data. The dependent variable was ordinarily the change in the number of average weekly plant hours from 1929 to 1976. Some thought was given to analyzing changes in the number

---

[5] Jorgenson and Griliches noted the lack of an explicit theory of capital utilization. See "Issues in Growth Accounting: A Reply to Edward F. Denison," *Survey of Current Business*, vol. 52, no. 5 (May 1972), part II. I understand that Betancourt and Clague have developed a growth model that embodies utilization in their forthcoming book.

of shifts over time, but this was rejected because hours per shift have changed over time.

Continuous Operations. Within industries the rise in the proportion of output produced through continuous operations should help explain part of the rise in average weekly plant hours from 1929 to 1976. This study first ruled out those industries that were completely continuous in both years. Two measures of continuousness were then used. One used the employment data from the Census Bureau, which made it possible to calculate the share of industry employment accounted for by continuous plants in both 1929 and 1976. At a given time, ratios based on employment are biased downward compared with similar ratios based on output. The second measure was a dummy variable that indicated the presence or absence of a single plant operating 150 hours per week or more. The use of a single plant as a criterion for an entire industry has an obvious limitation. On the other hand, industries having only a single plant operating continuously may also embrace several plants of which parts operate continuously.

Current data show that only a fraction of shiftwork is continuous in most industries. Consequently it is necessary to look elsewhere for factors explaining the long-term rise in average weekly plant hours.

Capital Intensity and Its Trend. A cursory examination of the current Census Bureau surveys suggests that plants in capital-intensive industries work the longest hours and that plants in labor-intensive industries work the shortest. This is in accord with theory and with the findings of investigators in foreign countries. Since an increase in capital intensity is an incentive to adopt multiple-shift work, those industries in which capital intensity has increased most should show the greatest increase in average weekly plant hours.

Capital intensity has been measured in many ways. The theory of shift work suggests that the proper measure is a comparison (over time) of instantaneous ratios of capital costs to combined capital and labor costs on a one-shift basis for new plants, appropriately deflated.[6] At the detailed industry level, the measurement of capital intensity runs into serious difficulties. To be sure, for recent years data are available from the Census Bureau on the book value (historical cost) of gross fixed assets for four-digit industries. Estimates of gross and net fixed assets in 1972 prices have been published by the Bureau of Labor Statistics at the three-digit level for the years 1947 through

---

[6] Betancourt and Clague, "An Economic Analysis of Capital Utilization," pp. 69-78.

1974. For 1929, however, Creamer's estimates of net fixed assets in constant prices exist only for a little more than two-digit industry detail.[7]

Census data made possible the calculation of ratios of horsepower (a proxy for fixed assets) to wage earner man-hours by detailed industry for 1929 and 1962, the last year for which horsepower statistics are available. These 1962 figures were spliced to ratios of fixed assets (in 1972 prices) to production worker man-hours, which were calculated for 1974 as well as for 1962. Obviously these yielded only rough approximations of the change in the ratio of capital stock to man-hours. It was especially troubling that the capital stock or its proxy, horsepower, was related to man-hours of workers on *all* shifts and that capital intensity so measured could not differentiate between an industry working one shift and an industry with the same capital working three shifts. In spite of its limitations I finally decided to use as the measure of capital intensity the ratio of kilowatt-hours of all electricity consumed to wage earner man-hours. The kilowatt-hours of electricity consumed could be a proxy for machine hours or capital services. All the data are available from Census of Manufactures sources.[8]

Wage Differentials for Late-Shift Work. Studies by the Bureau of Labor Statistics have demonstrated some important facts about shift

---

[7] Daniel Creamer, Sergei Dobrovolsky, and Israel Borenstein, *Capital in Manufacturing and Mining: Its Formation and Financing* (Princeton, N.J.: Princeton University Press for National Bureau of Economic Research, 1960).

[8] Electricity is used in factories for driving motors, for lighting, for heat-treating furnaces, in electrochemical processes, and for space heating and cooling. For most industries, however, driving motors is by far the most important use. For a fuller discussion of this use of electricity consumption, see Murray F. Foss, "The Utilization of Capital Equipment," *Survey of Current Business*, vol. 43, no. 6 (June 1963), pp. 8-16.

Total electricity consumed in 1929 was obtained by adding to the data on purchased electricity by industry, published in the 1929 Census of Manufactures, estimates of electricity generated by the plant itself. Data for 1929 on electricity generated by manufacturing plants were collected in the 1929 census but were never published. I used the (blown-up) sample of the 1929 census to obtain ratios of purchased electricity to total electricity consumed by industry and then used those ratios with published data on purchased electricity to obtain total electricity consumed by industry. Strictly speaking, an allowance should be made for electricity generated by the plant and sold to outsiders, but such information was not collected in 1929.

Since the pronounced increase in the price of electricity starting in 1974, manufacturing plants have taken steps to economize on electricity consumption, so that the use of kilowatt-hours as a proxy for machine hours may have suffered. To this extent the 1976 ratios of kilowatt-hours to man-hours may be distorted. Because only a few years are involved (1974 through 1976), the changes from 1929 to 1976 are probably not affected very much.

TABLE 19
Wage Differentials for Second-Shift Work Compared with Average Hourly Earnings in Manufacturing, 1961 and 1976

	Gross Average Hourly Earnings Excluding Overtime	Second-Shift Differential	Differential as Percent of Gross Earnings
1961	$2.25	$0.104	4.6
1976	5.02	0.205	4.1

Source: Calculations in second and third columns by author. Gross average hourly earnings apply to the entire United States as shown in U.S. Department of Labor, Bureau of Labor Statistics, *Employment and Earnings* (August 1980), p. 81. Second-shift differential applies to metropolitan areas as shown in U.S. Department of Labor, Bureau of Labor Statistics, *Area Wage Statistics: Metropolitan Areas, United States and Regional Summaries,* Bulletin 1900-82, 1979, p. 91.

differentials that are especially relevant to this study. First, wage differentials for late shifts are not large in relation to first-shift wages in U.S. manufacturing, and, second, shift differentials have not kept pace with the general rise of wages in manufacturing.[9] Table 19 provides some overall figures for manufacturing. The relative decline in the differential is more than just a mix effect, since slower rates of increase in shift differentials relative to wage rates have generally been observed in specific industries. Table 20 provides an example from the printing trades. Theory suggests that at a particular time the smaller the wage differential for late-shift work, the greater the incentive for the firm to use shift work. Over time, a relative decline in the night wage differential could be a factor facilitating the rise in shift work. It turned out that measuring this variable by industry was difficult, so it is taken up in a separate section.

Even though it is beyond the scope of this particular study, it is interesting to speculate further about the long-term rise in shift work and the apparent failure of shift differentials to keep pace with the general rise in wages. Taken together, these developments suggest that the supply curve of labor willing to work at night may have shifted outward. Such a movement of the supply curve may reflect a number of factors affecting individuals' welfare. For example, night work may be less distasteful today because transportation costs in time and effort are lower as a result of better automobiles and

---

[9] See especially Charles W. O'Connor, "Late-Shift Employment in Manufacturing Industries," *Monthly Labor Review,* vol. 93, no. 11 (November 1970), pp. 37-42.

TABLE 20

WAGE DIFFERENTIALS FOR NIGHT WORK ON NEWSPAPERS AS PERCENT OF
DAY WORK RATE: SELECTED UNION PRINTING TRADES, 1929 AND 1976

Trade	1929	1976
Compositor	10.2	3.9
Machine tender (machinist)	13.0	3.3
Machine operator	9.2	6.0
Photoengraver	18.6	4.3
Pressman (web presses)	15.4	7.4
Stereotyper	13.8	10.7

SOURCE: Calculations by author based on U.S. Department of Labor, Bureau of
Labor Statistics, *Union Wages and Hours: Printing Industry, July 1, 1976,* Bulletin
1986, p. 13, and comparable data for 1929.

highways or because amenities in factories have been improved. The
movement of the curve could reflect alternative family arrangements
in which a mother works on a day shift and a father on a night shift.
Certain locational influences may be operating. It may be that
decisions by business on where to locate new multishift plants have
been significantly influenced by the availability of a labor supply willing to work late shifts at relatively low wage differentials; this could
be true when plants were located in rural areas—or at least away
from large cities—and represented opportunities for farmers either
to quit farming or to moonlight and thus improve their real wage as
compared with real wages in farming. If this were the case, increases
in shift work at relatively low wages in rural areas could be an important nexus between capital investment and the movement of labor
out of farming. Denison attached importance to the shift of farm
labor to nonfarm employment in accounting for the growth in total
output since 1929.[10]

Women in the Labor Supply. If women are the main source of added
labor supply and women cannot or do not wish to work at night,
industries may find themselves less able to use shift work. Institutional and legal factors may also limit shift work. In 1937, for
example, sixteen states prohibited night work for women, although
in at least three states the prohibitions did not apply to manufacturing.

[10] Edward F. Denison, *Accounting for United States Economic Growth 1929-1969*
(Washington, D.C.: Brookings Institution, 1974).

Massachusetts prohibited work by women in textile and leather plants from 6 P.M. to 6 A.M., but the period during which night work was most commonly prohibited was from 10 P.M. to 6 A.M.[11] In the late 1960s there were still some states that prohibited or regulated night work by women, although the number was falling rapidly as a result of the movement toward equality of the sexes.[12] The proportion of women in total employment should be inversely related to the length of the plant workweek, certainly for 1929. Because of the movement toward equality of the sexes, the expected relationship in 1976 and the expected relationship between the change in the women's share of employment and the change in plant hours are uncertain. The Bureau of Labor Statistics publishes current data that permit the calculation of the proportion that women constitute of total employment in various industries; similar data are available from the 1929 Census of Manufactures.

The Effect of the Wage-Hour Law. The passage of the Fair Labor Standards Act in 1938 (the wage-hour law) probably had a perceptible influence on the adoption of multiple-shift work because of the statutory requirement that overtime be paid at time and a half. Other things equal, the longer the typical workweek of *labor* before the passage of the new legislation, the greater the incentive for an industry to switch to shift work. The length of the labor workweek in 1929 was taken as an indication of its length at the time the wage-hour law was passed. This is an obvious simplification since hours fell during the 1930s. Also it should be noted that the forty-hour week for labor did not become operative in manufacturing until 1940, even though the law was passed in 1938. Data on the workweek of labor by detailed industry, measured by "prevailing" hours, can be closely approximated from tables published in the 1929 Census of Manufactures.

Virtually all industries grew from 1929 to 1976, and most grew substantially. Presumably industries had the choice of expanding via one-shift operations in larger plants. This hypothesis suggests that the industries that adapted most rapidly to the forty-hour labor week by means of multiple shifts, that is, long *plant* hours, were those that started off with long *labor* hours and a large potential liability as a result of the wage-hour legislation.

---

[11] U.S. Department of Labor, Bureau of Labor Statistics, *State Labor Laws for Women*, Bulletin of the Women's Bureau, No. 156, 1938, pp. 3-6.

[12] O'Connor, "Late-Shift Employment," p. 42, fn. 5.

Management Limitations. Data from the current Census Bureau survey indicate that average weekly plant hours are least in industries in which the size of establishments is small. As noted earlier, a few industries, such as apparel and footwear, operate their plants fewer hours today than they did in 1929. These are industries in which owners may provide a significant share of total labor input or may constitute the only managerial input available to the firm. The owner may feel that his presence is always needed and may balk at working the long hours required for, say, two shifts, preferring leisure over additional income.[13] Not only is management a factor limiting shift work, but its influence should be expected to diminish over time, since small firms have decreased in relative importance within industries. This variable is measured by the proportion of output (value added) accounted for by single-plant companies. Data came from the 1929 and 1972 Censuses of Manufactures. The use of 1972 rather than 1976 should have very small effects on the results. Also considered was an alternative version of this variable—the share of industry output accounted for by noncorporate business—but in the end this version was not used because the noncorporate form of organization does not quite capture the concept of smallness being investigated here.

Regression Results

Before the analysis of factors accounting for the change in average weekly plant hours among industries from 1929 to 1976, an attempt was made to explain the variation in average weekly plant hours at points in time—1929 and 1976. Each year was analyzed separately by means of the same independent variables where possible.

The industries examined in both the cross-sectional and change versions of the study were those that could be matched in both years, either directly or through combination. By "matched" I mean producing the same or similar products. On this basis there were approximately ninety four-digit industries or groups of industries. They are shown in appendix F, which also discusses some of the problems of classification.

It might be argued that limiting the study to industries or industry groups that could be matched over almost half a century is bound to give biased results in the sense that these groups must necessarily

---

[13] This fits in with Scitovsky's point that entrepreneurs are not solely profits maximizers but may also be affected by considerations of leisure. See T. Scitovsky, "A Note on Profit Maximization and Its Implications," *Review of Economic Studies*, vol. 11 (1943), pp. 57-60. I am indebted to Mickey Levy of the American Enterprise Institute for calling this to my attention.

omit new products not produced in the earlier period and older products no longer being produced. This is a possibility. The unweighted average change in weekly plant hours from 1929 to 1976 for more than ninety matched industries or industry groups was 33 percent (median 29 percent), which is above the weighted changes for all manufacturing combined shown in the last column of table 4.

Cross-section Equations. The independent variables analyzed for the year 1976 were (1) capital intensity, measured by the ratio of kilowatt-hours to man-hours, (2) percentage of value added accounted for by single-unit companies (SUVA), (3) percentage of employment accounted for by women, (4) continuousness, (5) percentage of production workers unionized, and (6) capacity utilization.

A word about variables (5) and (6), which have not been discussed. Freeman and Medoff recently published some cross-sectional data on the proportion of production workers covered by collective bargaining agreements at the three-digit industry level and applicable to the years 1968 to 1972.[14] The difference in years as compared with 1976 is probably not serious, because the degree of unionization in an industry is not likely to change much over a period of a few years, but applying proportions found in three-digit industries to four-digit industries may not be valid. An example of a pure union effect would be prohibitions of shift work by union workers such as those found in certain apparel industries and among retail meatcutters. To this extent the degree of unionization and the length of the plant workweek should be negatively related. The share of industry employment that is unionized, however, may also reflect such things as capital intensity or a large wage differential for late-shift work. The other additional variable being discussed refers to percentage of capacity utilization in the fourth quarter of 1976. This information was taken from the same basic Census Bureau survey used for average weekly plant hours. This variable could pick up some of the response to short-run fluctuations in demand encountered by various industries and thus might account for some of the variations in average weekly plant hours in the fourth quarter of 1976.

The results of two equations based on ordinary least squares are shown in table 21. Somewhat better results are obtained in the equation employing the dummy for continuousness. In this equation coefficients of three of the six variables are significant at the .05 level: continuousness, percentage of value added in single-unit companies,

[14] Richard Freeman and James Medoff, "New Estimates of Private Sector Unionism in the United States," *Industrial and Labor Relations Review*, vol. 32, no. 2 (January 1979).

TABLE 21

REGRESSION COEFFICIENTS OF EQUATIONS EXPLAINING 1976 AVERAGE WEEKLY PLANT HOURS WITH TWO VARIANTS FOR CONTINUOUSNESS VARIABLE

	Using Dummy for Continuousness		Using Percentage for Continuousness	
Constant	39.83	(0.8)	48.76	(1.0)
Variables				
Capital intensity	0.3789 (5.4)[a]		0.3383 (3.8)[a]	
SUVA[b]	−0.5097 (4.3)[a]		−0.5653 (4.5)[a]	
Women	−0.0022 (0.0)		−0.0449 (0.4)	
Continuousness	15.9513 (3.6)[a]		0.2359 (1.6)	
Unionization	0.0469 (0.5)		0.0570 (0.6)	
Capacity utilization	0.3772 (0.7)		0.3500 (0.6)	
R^2	0.62		0.57	
N	85		85	

NOTE: t-statistics are shown in parentheses.
[a] Significant at the .05 level.
[b] Percent of value added accounted for by single-unit companies.

and capital intensity. The signs of these coefficients, including the negative sign for percentage of value added in single-unit companies, turn out as expected.

In the companion equation, the continuousness variable does not pass the t-test at .05. An examination of the correlation matrix reveals a high correlation ($r = 0.6$) between continuousness measured in this fashion and the capital intensity variable; this is substantially greater than in the alternative version.

Substituting weekly plant hours at preferred rates of capacity utilization as an alternative measure of the dependent variable did not yield results much different from those based on actual hours of operation in 1976.

To explain variations in average weekly plant hours in 1929, I used the same independent variables as in 1976 but was unable to test the unionization and capacity utilization variables because data were not available. Table 22 gives results based on two variants of the continuousness variable. This time the equation measuring continuousness as a percentage yields the higher R^2, but at 0.50 it is lower than either version of the 1976 results. In this 1929 equation, only two variables are significant at the .05 level: percent of value added

TABLE 22
REGRESSION COEFFICIENTS OF EQUATIONS EXPLAINING 1929 AVERAGE
WEEKLY PLANT HOURS WITH TWO VARIANTS FOR
CONTINUOUSNESS VARIABLE

	Using Dummy for Continuousness		Using Percentage for Continuousness	
Constant	70.46	(13.4)[a]	70.51	(14.4)[a]
Variables				
Capital intensity	0.7205	(2.2)[a]	0.3805	(1.2)
SUVA[b]	−0.2356	(3.2)[a]	−0.2161	(3.2)[a]
Women	−0.1321	(1.6)	−0.1187	(1.5)
Continuousness	24.02	(4.6)[a]	1.3642	(6.0)[a]
R^2	0.43		0.50	
N	91		91	

NOTE: t-statistics are shown in parentheses.
[a] Significant at the .05 level.
[b] Percent of value added accounted for by single-unit companies.

in single-unit companies and percent of employment accounted for by continuous plants. The former variable has the correct negative sign. In the same equation, the capital intensity variable did not pass the t-test at the .05 level. The correlation between it and continuousness is somewhat high ($r = 0.4$). The coefficient on the proportion of women in total employment is negative and appears to have much more significance than in 1976, although it is not significant at the .05 level.

The 1976 equations were then rerun so that the independent variables used for the 1976 and 1929 cross-sectional versions would be identical (table 23).

Changes, 1929–1976. The discussion has dealt with cross-sectional regressions applicable to 1976 and 1929, but my main interest centers on the behavior of these variables when measured in terms of their change from 1929 to 1976. The change version used as a dependent variable the absolute (rather than percentage) increase or decrease in average weekly plant hours from 1929 to 1976. The independent variables were absolute changes over the same time period in (1) capital intensity, as measured by the ratio of kilowatt-hours to man-hours, (2) the proportion of value added accounted for by single-unit companies, (3) the share of women in total employment, and (4) continuousness. The final independent variable measures the length

TABLE 23

Regression Coefficients of Equations Explaining Average Weekly Plant Hours with Two Variants for Continuousness Variable, 1929 and 1976

	Using Dummy for Continuousness				Using Percentage for Continuousness			
	1929		1976		1929		1976	
Constant	70.46	(13.4)	77.00	(14.6)	70.51	(14.4)	83.98	(16.3)
Variables								
Capital intensity	0.7205	(2.2)	0.4029	(6.0)	0.3805	(1.2)	0.3627	(4.2)
SUVA[a]	−0.2356	(3.2)	−0.4912	(4.4)	−0.2161	(3.2)	−0.5528	(4.8)
Women	−0.1321	(1.6)	−0.0030	(0.0)	−0.1187	(1.5)	−0.0471	(0.5)
Continuousness	24.02	(4.6)	15.73	(3.6)	1.3642	(6.0)	0.23	(1.6)
R^2	0.43		0.60		0.50		0.55	
N	91		90		91		90	

NOTE: t-statistics are shown in parentheses.

[a] Percent of value added accounted for by single-unit companies.

of the labor workweek in 1929 in excess of forty hours. Note that the reduction in the length of the labor week from before the wage-hour law to after the wage-hour law is shown as a positive number and should be positively correlated with the increase in plant hours.

Table 24 presents the results of the change equations with two versions for continuousness. The version employing the dummy variable for continuousness does much better than the one using the percentage, although neither is very high. With the former, the coefficients on variables for capital intensity, single-unit value added, continuousness, and labor workweek have the correct signs, and all are significant at the .05 level. The coefficient for the share of women in total employment is significant at the .10 level. There was some uncertainty about the sign of this coefficient. The negative suggests that the rise in the women's share of employment has had the effect of holding down weekly plant hours. The comparatively low t-values for capital intensity and continuousness when continuousness is measured as a percentage are attributable to multicollinearity. For these two variables, $r = 0.6$. In this version the coefficient on women becomes somewhat more significant than in the other version.

The coefficient on weekly labor hours in 1929 indicates that, for every hour by which the workweek of labor in 1929 exceeded

TABLE 24
Regression Coefficients of Equations Explaining the Change in Average Weekly Plant Hours from 1929 to 1976, with Two Variants for Continuousness Variable

	Using Dummy for Continuousness		Using Percentage for Continuousness	
Constant	−10.54	(1.2)	−10.83	(1.2)
Variables				
Capital intensity	0.2434 (2.3)[a]		0.1951 (1.4)	
SUVA[c]	−0.2354 (2.0)[a]		−0.2503 (2.0)[a]	
Women	−0.3036 (1.8)[b]		−0.3569 (2.1)[a]	
Continuousness	13.04	(3.0)[a]	0.1716 (0.9)	
Labor workweek in 1929	1.96	(2.6)[a]	2.23	(2.9)[a]
R^2	0.28		0.21	
N	88		88	

NOTE: t-statistics are shown in parentheses.
[a] Significant at .05 level.
[b] Significant at .10 level.
[c] Percent of value added accounted for by single-unit companies.

forty, the length of the plant workweek increased by 2.0 to 2.2 hours from 1929 to 1976.

Wage Differentials for Late-Shift Work. Although the Bureau of Labor Statistics has published a fairly large body of data on the prevalence and size of shift differentials by industry, not much direct information is available for years before World War II. One limited source of such information consists of the wage chronologies maintained by the bureau for particular unions and companies. All the chronologies have sections dealing with shift differentials, but an examination of nineteen agreements with beginning dates ranging from 1936 to 1943 revealed few provisions for shift premium pay. Of eight agreements with beginning dates before 1940, only two provided for shift premium pay. Since it is more likely that shift differentials would be found in contracts between large unions and large companies than in small companies or nonunion firms, the evidence from the wage chronologies suggests that shift differentials were at best uncommon in 1929. A notable exception was the printing industry, some data for which were presented in table 20. Shift differentials were provided in agreements in several major defense industries in 1940 and increased in importance during World War II.[15] Since then they have become common if not large. Albert Rees has pointed out that even among unions shift differentials are relatively small, because late-shift workers tend to be those with the least seniority or at the greatest disadvantage in the labor market.[16]

Testing the current effect of the wage differential on weekly plant hours was limited by the small number of industries providing shift differential data for very recent years. Nineteen industries or groups of industries provided such information. The shift differential was measured by the ratio of the dollars-and-cents differential for the second shift to straight-time earnings for the industry times the fraction of employment in plants paying the differential. Thus a 6 percent differential paid by plants whose employment was 50 percent of estimated total industry employment was reduced to 3 percent.

According to theory, the higher the shift differential, the less the likelihood that the firm will resort to extra shifts. But it is also clear that the higher the shift differential for working evenings and nights, the greater the supply of labor that will be forthcoming. Since the wage differential affects both supply and demand, what is required is a model with both a supply and a demand equation. In the model that follows, average weekly plant hours (WEPLHRS) are a function of supply (1) and demand (2):

(1) WEPLHRS = f(women, unionization, shift differential)
(2) WEPLHRS = g(capital/labor, continuousness, percent of output in single-unit firms, shift differential)

The third equation sets supply equal to demand. Solving the model by two-stage least squares gives the results in table 25 for 1976.

The coefficient for the shift differential has a negative sign in the demand equation and a positive sign in the supply equation, but the coefficients have low t-values. Indeed, none of the coefficients in the demand equation has an acceptable t-statistic, and for some variables the sign is wrong.

It could be argued that the shift differential by itself is so small that it cannot constitute much of an attraction for workers who have alternative employment opportunities at the first-shift wage. If they do not have these opportunities, however, the wage itself—aside from the differential—might be an attraction, as Rees has suggested. This could be the case with farmers, women, and minorities for whom alternatives to shift work are low-paying work, such as farm work, or even unemployment. Consequently, in the model just described, the

---

[15] Frederick Mueller and James Nix, "Premium Pay: An Analysis of Industrial Practices," *Monthly Labor Review* (August 1951), pp. 148-151.

[16] Albert Rees, *The Economics of Work and Pay*, 2d ed. (New York: Harper & Row, 1979), p. 29.

TABLE 25

Regression Coefficients of Model Explaining Average Weekly Plant Hours in 1976 Using Shift Differential

	Supply Equation	Demand Equation
Constant	14.09	240.6
Variables		
Shift differential	2.992	−30.25
Capital intensity	—	0.89
SUVA[a]	—	−2.77
Women	1.35[b]	—
Continuousness (dummy)	—	−12.48
Unionization	0.47	—
N	19	19

[a] Percent of value added accounted for by single-unit companies.
[b] Significant at .05 level.

wage itself—measured by average hourly earnings from the census—was substituted for the shift differential. This information, unlike the shift differential data, is available for all industries.

Results of this formulation are shown in table 26 on the basis of eighty-seven industry observations for the year 1976. In the demand equation, all variables are highly significant except wages, which also have the wrong sign. In the supply equation the average wage has a positive sign and is significant. Finally, the unionization variable is negative but is significant only at a low level. A similar model for 1929 yielded coefficients on wages with the wrong sign in both the supply and demand equations.

This experiment with the wage data yielded disappointing results but touches on an interesting area and warrants greater attention. There are several reasons why average hourly earnings in an industry do not perform well. Strictly speaking one wants to hold occupation, experience, et cetera, constant in comparing one industry's wages with those of another. In the demand equation, wages and capital intensity are subject to a good deal of multicollinearity. The analysis should be aided by expanding the number of industries with shift differentials as well as taking account of differentials for third-shift work.

Plant Size. The tabulations presented earlier showed a positive relation between average weekly plant hours and size measured by value added per establishment in both 1976 and 1929. Not much time was devoted to the size variable, because it is closely associated (negatively) with the percent of output produced in single-plant companies.

TABLE 26
REGRESSION COEFFICIENTS OF MODEL EXPLAINING AVERAGE WEEKLY PLANT HOURS IN 1976 USING AVERAGE WAGE

	Supply Equation	Demand Equation
Constant	−128.4 [a]	72.91 [a]
Variables		
Average wage	36.61 [a]	0.76
Capital intensity	—	0.40 [a]
SUVA [b]	—	−0.47 [a]
Women	1.02 [a]	—
Continuousness (dummy)	—	15.24 [a]
Unionization	−0.23	—
N	87	87

[a] Significant at .05 level.
[b] Percent of value added accounted for by single-unit companies.

To a lesser extent there is a positive association between capital intensity and size, although this is true also of capital intensity and single-plant companies. Since there may be some interest in a simple size variable and its relationship with weekly plant hours, value added per establishment was calculated as shown in the Census of Manufactures for 1929 and 1972 (for the 1976 data) and was substituted for percent of value added in single-unit companies. The effects on the coefficient of determination are mixed, as the data in the first two columns of table 27 indicate, but reasons for the considerable improvement in 1929 are not obvious. Putting both variables into the same equation does not increase the explained variance by much because of multicollinearity.

TABLE 27
COMPARISON OF VALUES OF R^2 AMONG EQUATIONS UTILIZING DIFFERENT MEASURES OF SIZE

	Value Added in Single-Unit Firms	Value Added per Establishment	Both Variables in Same Equation
Cross section			
1929	0.43 [a]	0.58	0.59
1976	0.60 [a]	0.58	0.62
Change, 1929 to 1976	0.28 [b]	0.24	—

[a] See table 23 with dummy for continuousness variable.
[b] See table 24 with dummy for continuousness variable.

4
Concluding Remarks

This study has focused on two things: On the basis of some new information it has compared the workweek of fixed capital in the mid-1970s with the workweek in 1929, and it has made a start in analyzing why the change has occurred. The economic significance of a long-term rise in average weekly hours worked by capital has already been discussed, but other implications are worth noting.

Construction. It is reasonable to suppose that a lengthening in factory hours will bring about relatively greater savings in plant costs than in equipment costs, because user-cost depreciation and maintenance charges vary more closely with use for equipment than for plant. If this is so, the rise in average weekly plant hours could help explain the small rise in plant as compared with equipment in the manufacturing sector from 1929 to 1976. Over this period the stock of plant construction increased by only 57 percent, compared with a rise of 404 percent in the stock of equipment, according to estimates by the Bureau of Economic Analysis. It is very likely, however, that other influences are at work here. For example, the more rapid rise in plant than in equipment costs may have favored substitution of equipment for plant.

Energy. The energy crisis brings several crosscurrents affecting use of capital. Sharply higher energy costs since the end of 1973 may be causing manufacturing firms to substitute labor for capital. If this is so—and it is still a matter of considerable controversy among economists—it would be a reversal of the long-term trend and could lead to shorter plant hours.[17] On the other hand, some electric

---

[17] Edward A. Hudson and Dale W. Jorgenson, "The Economic Impact of Policies to Reduce U.S. Energy Growth," *Resources and Energy*, vol. 1 (1978), pp. 205-229. Also Ernest R. Berndt and David O. Wood, "Engineering and Econometric Interpretations of Energy-Capital Complementarity," *American Economic Review*, vol. 69, no. 3 (June 1979), pp. 342-354.

utilities are advocating "time of day" pricing, which offers lower rates for electricity used at night, when demand is lower.[18] This kind of pricing could encourage more shift work. The net result of these opposing influences cannot be determined at this time.

Age of Capital. The findings of this study have implications regarding the age of the capital stock and how it is used up. Analysts of economic growth disagree among themselves not only about the role of capital utilization in economic growth but also about which measure of capital is most appropriate to calculate the change in capital input.[19] Frequently estimates of the gross stock of capital are built up by the "perpetual inventory" method, which requires estimates of past investment flows, of survival rates as reflected in data on average useful lives of fixed assets, and of distributions around the averages. Stock estimates of this type are synthetic series that serve in the absence of directly observable data.

Treasury Department studies made in the mid-1950s found that after World War II taxpayers were using shorter average useful lives for claiming depreciation on equipment than those shown in Bulletin F, published in January 1942.[20] The Treasury Department did not offer reasons for the decline. Bert Hickman suggested that Bulletin F reflected the "average experience of the 1930s with its low standards of obsolescence."[21] As Hickman noted, although the Treasury published Bulletin F as a guide to businessmen for calculating depreciation, it has not viewed useful lives in Bulletin F as binding if taxpayers could demonstrate that their fixed assets have shorter useful lives.

Average useful lives as claimed for tax purposes have continued to fall. Most investigators seem to agree that actual useful lives—as distinct from those used for tax purposes—have not fallen as much, and indeed, there is some question whether actual lives have fallen at

---

[18] Joann S. Lublin, "Blues in the Night," *Wall Street Journal*, October 18, 1977, p. 1. Also Lawrence Rout, "Environmentalists Are Split over Issue of Time-of-Day Pricing of Electricity," *Wall Street Journal*, October 15, 1978, p. 14.

[19] Denison, *Accounting for United States Economic Growth, 1929-1969*, pp. 63 and 284.

[20] Bulletin F average service lives for all manufacturing were nineteen years, whereas the survey average (based on a harmonic mean) was fifteen years. See Norman B. Ture, *Accelerated Depreciation in the United States, 1954-1960* (New York: Columbia University Press for National Bureau of Economic Research, 1967), table C-4. See also U.S. Treasury Department, Internal Revenue Service, Bulletin F, January 1942; and U.S. Treasury Department, Internal Revenue Service, *Life of Depreciable Assets Source Book*.

[21] Bert G. Hickman, *Investment Demand and U.S. Economic Growth* (Washington, D.C.: Brookings Institution, 1965).

all. That they have declined in fact is mainly an inference from the behavior of tax lives, although it should be noted that Treasury Department estimates in the early 1960s of actual service lives for manufacturing were also below those of Bulletin F.[22]

A rise in shift work, much of which may have occurred in the 1940s and 1950s, could help explain the apparent drop in average useful lives of equipment and could shed some light on the problem of the measurement of actual or economic depreciation. In the measurement of capital inputs, knowledge of the prevalence of shift work and its development would help the analyst in the choice of the many stock series now in existence. In this connection it is of interest that, in its estimates of capital stocks, the Bureau of Economic Analysis has long calculated one variant in which average useful lives remain at Bulletin F values up to 1940, decline gradually to 75 percent of Bulletin F values by 1960, and remain at 75 percent thereafter. This variant is not inconsistent with the findings of this study and the conjectures offered here regarding the post-1929 development of shift work.

Agenda for Further Research

1. This study should help fill a gap that had been noted by earlier investigators of capital and its role in the growth of the U.S. economy. Whether the findings presented here for manufacturing are valid for the rest of the economy remains to be seen. Furthermore, as already indicated, there is reason to believe that the trend to shift work in manufacturing at least did not proceed smoothly but was accentuated during World War II and the early postwar years. Research aimed at estimating the workweek of capital in nonmanufacturing industries and for periods of time between 1929 and 1976 is now under way. Once the picture is more complete it should be possible to reevaluate for the entire business economy the role of the growth of capital and of total factor productivity in a growth accounting framework.

2. The findings of this study confirm at least two suggestions put forth in the author's 1963 article, which showed an increase of some 50 percent in the relative utilization of equipment in manufacturing from 1929 to the mid-1950s.[23] The earlier article suggested —but provided no supporting evidence—that the rise in the relative utilization of equipment was due to a number of factors, among them a trend to shift work, a trend to continuous operations, and greater

---

[22] Hickman, *Investment Demand*, and Ture, *Accelerated Depreciation*, table C-4.
[23] Foss, "Utilization of Capital Equipment."

efficiency in the use of equipment by management when shift work is held constant. Since longer capital hours due to increased shift work show some relation to changes in total factor productivity, there is reason to believe that increased utilization of capital because of efforts by management to become more efficient—aside from shift work—will show similar results. Indeed, it is possible that the two influences combined have been of genuine importance in accounting for the growth in total factor productivity in manufacturing.

3. There should be further study of geographical and locational factors in explaining the rise of shift work. The broad patterns already discussed suggest that regions had a significant influence on plant hours in 1929 that has been considerably diminished since then. Was shift work more prevalent in the South and West and less so in the Northeast because the supply of capital was limited in the less industrialized regions and plentiful in the industrial Northeast? Or was this more of a reflection of institutional factors such as laws regulating the working conditions of women and a desire of business to avoid unionization?

Locational influences may reflect the effect of size of community on wages, shift differentials, degree of unionization, etc. Earlier discussion referred to the process by which firms located new plants in rural areas and small towns and tapped a large potential labor supply engaged in lower-paying farm work. The process by which labor shifted from farms to nonfarm work is worth exploring, given its importance in the nation's growth. It seems to be intimately bound up with investment and the growth of capital inputs.

4. More work should be done on the relationship between shift differentials and the prevalence of shift work. The small amount of work done in the present study was limited by availability of shift differential data and by the absence of time series on weekly plant hours.

5. Recently published data from the Labor Department suggest above average proportions of blacks and other minorities as compared with whites on evening and night shifts.[24] Does work on late shifts at relatively low shift differentials represent some form of discrimination?

6. Has the pace of technological change had an effect on the adoption of shift work? Other things equal, the more rapid the rate of technological change, the greater the incentive to use up plant and equipment—in the physical sense—in a given time period. The

---

[24] Janice N. Hedges and Edward S. Sekscenski, "Workers on Late Shifts in a Changing Economy," *Monthly Labor Review*, vol. 102 (September 1979), pp. 14-22.

adoption of shift work should be one way of accomplishing this objective.

7. What was the trend of factory hours of operation before 1929? Earlier in this century we find references to the need for multiple-shift operations as a condition for rising living standards. As Alfred Marshall stated:

> The importance of this consideration [of higher utilization] is more apparent every year, since the growing expensiveness of machinery and the quickness with which it is rendered obsolete are constantly increasing the wastefulness of keeping the untiring iron and steel resting in idleness during sixteen hours out of the twenty-four.[25]

Was the 1929 condition the outgrowth of earlier developments? It has been suggested that, in the very early days of the factory system, capital was operated extremely long hours but that, over the latter part of the nineteenth century and the early twentieth century—when capital-output ratios in U.S. manufacturing were rising—hours worked by capital were cut by social legislation and by the rise of trade unions, developments that put limits on the workweek of labor.

---

[25] Marshall, *Principles of Economics* (9th ed., variorum), cited in Winston, "The Theory of Capital Utilization and Idleness," *Journal of Economic Literature*, vol. 12, no. 4 (December 1974), p. 1309.

Appendix A

Survey of Plant Capacity

The following form was used by the Bureau of the Census in conducting the survey of plant capacity.

Appendix A

Form Approved: O.M.B. No. 41-R2806

FORM **MQ-C1**
(12-10-76)

U.S. DEPARTMENT OF COMMERCE
BUREAU OF THE CENSUS

SURVEY OF PLANT CAPACITY

FOURTH QUARTER 1976

RETURN TO → Bureau of the Census
1201 East Tenth Street
Jeffersonville, Indiana 47132

Please READ carefully the specific instructions with each item on the reverse side before filling this report.

NOTICE — Response to this inquiry is required by law (title 13, U.S. Code). By the same law, your report to the Census Bureau is confidential. It may be seen only by sworn Census employees and may be used only for statistical purposes. The law also provides that copies retained in your files are immune from legal process.

In correspondence pertaining to this report, refer to the file number above your name.

PLEASE RETURN THIS COPY
(Please correct any error in name and address including ZIP code)

GENERAL INSTRUCTIONS

Fourth Quarter 1976 (October-December) — Please complete the information requested for the establishment described in the address box of this form. If your company operates more than one manufacturing location, you are requested to report only for those specifically selected for this survey.

This report will be used to compile estimates of capacity by industry and for manufacturing as a whole in order to evaluate the actual performance of manufacturing in the months ahead. The information is of great value not only to the Bureau of the Census, but also to the Federal Reserve Board, Council of Economic Advisers, and other parts of the Government responsible for tracking the performance of the economy. It is recognized that many companies do not have records readily at hand to compile a precise measure of capacity. It is also recognized that estimated capacity may vary considerably with the product mix which may be subject to substantial short run variation in many establishments. However, past surveys conducted by the Bureau of the Census and discussions with many firms indicate that most firms can overcome these obstacles and estimate the capabilities of the plants reasonably accurately in terms of man-hours or another item such as output or materials put through.

We urge you to make a reasonable effort to complete the various sections of the report form. If you feel that you cannot complete the **Item 1 data** for production or materials, a man-hour estimate of preferred rate and practical capacity is acceptable.

Please use the remarks section to make comments about the method you used to obtain your estimate of capacity. Such comments will enhance the usefulness of the resulting data or will reduce questions we may have about your report.

Shifts Per Day — Most shifts are assumed to be of 8 hours duration so that a 3-shift operation is usually maximum. If you are operating with a variation that leads to more than three shifts or to fractional shifts, please use the remarks to explain briefly your operations.

Days Per Week and Hours Per Day — Refer to the duration the plant is open and operating, not to the man-hours put in by your work force.

Number of Production Workers and Total Man-hours — Should be the same as reported for this establishment on your 1976 Annual Survey of Manufactures Form MA-100 *(Items 2 and 4).*

Preferred Level of Operations — This is ordinarily an intermediate level of operations between actual operations and practical capacity which you would prefer not to exceed because of costs or other considerations (although in some instances it may be possible to prefer a higher level of operations than practical capacity would permit). If no such level exists as far as the plant operation is concerned, please enter "same as practical capacity" in item 1, column c.

Practical Capacity — This is the greatest level of output this plant can achieve within the framework of a realistic work pattern. In estimating practical capacity, please take into account the following considerations:

1. Assume a normal product mix. If the plant is subject to considerable short run variation in product mix you may assume that the current pattern of production is normal unless it is unusually different because of a unique situation in the 4th quarter 1976.

2. In setting capacity in terms of the number of shifts and hours of plant operation assume an expansion of operations that can be reasonably attained in your industry and your locality.

3. Consider only the machinery and equipment in place and ready to operate. Do not consider facilities which have been inoperative for a long period of time and, therefore, require extensive reconditioning before they can be made operative.

4. Take into account the additional downtime for maintenance, repair, or clean-up which would be required as you move from current operations to full capacity.

5. Assume availability of labor, materials, utilities, etc., sufficient to utilize the machinery and equipment that was in place at the end of the quarter.

6. Do not consider overtime pay, added costs for materials or other costs to be limiting factors in setting capacity.

7. Although it may be possible to expand plant output by using productive facilities outside of the plant, such as by contracting out subassembly work, do not assume the use of such outside facilities in more than the proportion that has been normal in your current level of operations.

1. ACTUAL, PREFERRED, AND PRACTICAL LEVELS OF OPERATIONS FOR FOURTH QUARTER 1976 (OCT.–DEC.) – In reporting shifts, days, and hours of operations you may use the most typical pattern during the period. **Lines 1 through 7** – Please make every effort to report information requested in columns (b), (c), and (d).

Line No.	Item (a)	4th Quarter 1976		
		Actual operations (b)	Preferred level of operations (c)	Practical capacity (d)
1	Shifts per day *(Number)*	1011	1012	1013
2	Days per week in operation *(Number)*	1021	1022	1023
3	Hours per day in operation *(Number)*	1031	1032	1033
4	Number of production workers as of November 12	1041	1042	1043
5	Total man-hours worked during the quarter by production workers *(Thousands)*	1051	1052	1053
6	Percent of overtime hours included in line 5	1061 %	1062 %	1063 %
7	Value of production *($1,000)*	1071	1072 $	1073 $
8	*If possible, please report for lines 8 and 9 below. Use reasonable estimates for the item(s) most suitable for your establishments.* Quantity of production – *Specify units*	1081	1082	1083
9	Quantity of materials consumed – *Specify units*	1091	1092	1093

2. OPERATING RATES DURING THE FOURTH QUARTER 1976

Line No.		Percent
1	At what percentage of practical capacity did this plant **actually** operate during the fourth quarter 1976?	2011 %
2	At what percentage of practical capacity would you have **preferred** this plant to operate during the fourth quarter 1976?	2012 %

3. REASONS FOR OPERATING AT LESS THAN 100% OF PRACTICAL CAPACITY AND LENGTH OF TIME REQUIRED TO REACH AND MAINTAIN PRACTICAL CAPACITY – If during the **4th quarter 1976** this establishment operated at less than 100% of your practical capacity, please report **3a, 3b, and 3c.**

a. Principal reason your operations fell short of practical capacity. Enter the number 1 through 6 for each applicable item to indicate the ranking of the reason in importance. *Number only those reasons which pertain to your operations.*

3011 _____ Insufficient orders

3014 _____ Lack of materials or supplies

3012 _____ Inadequate labor force (total or specific skills)

3015 _____ Strike or other work stoppages, etc.

3013 _____ Lack of sufficient fuel or electric energy

3016 _____ Other (fire, flood, etc.) – *Specify* _____

b. Length of time it would require to expand actual operations to practical capacity providing there was sufficient demand for the output *Mark (X) one*

3021 ☐ 1 week or less

3024 ☐ 4–6 months

3022 ☐ 2 weeks to a month

3025 ☐ More than 6 months – *Specify* _____

3023 ☐ 2–3 months

3026 ☐ Impractical to expand to practical capacity. *Specify estimated percent of practical capacity that could be reached within 6 months* . . . . [ ] %

61

Appendix A—Continued

c. Length of time practical level of operation could
be sustained (or level specified in 3026 above) . . . . 3031 ☐ Indefinitely   3032 ☐ Only _____ months
                                                                                                                      (Number)

Remarks

▶ 4. Person to contact regarding this report

Name	Title	Telephone		
		Area code	Number	Extension

Appendix B

Current Data: Qualifications, Survey Sample, and Estimating Procedure

The material in this appendix is taken directly from Census Bureau Form MQ-C1, Survey of Plant Capacity, fourth quarter 1976.

The survey estimates presented in this report are subject to both sampling and nonsampling errors. The nonsampling errors include various response and operational errors: errors of collection, reporting, transcription, errors due to nonresponse, etc. These errors would also occur if a complete canvass were to be conducted under the same conditions as this survey. It is believed that most of the important operational errors were detected and corrected in the course of the review of the data for reasonableness and consistency by the Bureau of the Census.

However, because of the definitional and conceptual problems associated with this survey, it is likely that the response errors are greater in magnitude than for other manufacturing surveys in which respondents are asked to report data that are generally kept as a matter of record. Explicit measures of the nonsampling errors are not available. As derived, the estimated standard errors, which are discussed below, include part of the effect of these nonsampling errors. The total error, though, will exceed the standard errors shown, and for particular estimates may exceed the standard errors by a considerable amount.

The particular sample selected for this survey is one of a large number of similar probability samples of the same size that could have been selected, by chance, using the same sample design. Each of the possible samples would yield somewhat different sets of results. The sampling errors—the differences between the estimates obtained and the results theoretically obtainable from a comparable complete canvass of the same target universe—is unknown. Guides to the potential size of the sampling errors, however, are provided by the estimated standard errors of the estimates.

In conjunction with its associated estimate, the estimate of standard error may be used to define confidence interval ranges which could be expected to include comparable complete coverage values for specified percentages of all possible samples. The complete coverage value would be included in the range:

1. From one standard error below to one standard error above the derived estimate for about two-thirds of all samples.

2. From two standard errors below to two standard errors above the derived estimate for about 19 out of 20 of all possible samples.

3. From three standard errors below to three standard errors above the derived estimate for nearly all samples.

An inference that the comparable complete coverage results would be within the indicated ranges would be correct in approximately the relative frequencies shown. Those proportions, therefore, may be interpreted as defining the confidence that the estimates shown would differ from complete coverage results by as much as one, two, or three standard errors, respectively.

For example, if an estimated utilization rate is shown as 80 percent with an associated standard error of 3 percent, then there is approximately 67 percent confidence that the interval 77 percent to 83 percent includes the complete coverage rate, about 95 percent confidence that the interval 74 percent to 86 percent inlcudes the complete coverage rate, and almost certain confidence that the interval 71 percent to 89 percent includes the complete coverage rate.

DESCRIPTION OF SURVEY SAMPLE AND ESTIMATING PROCEDURE

The estimates presented in this report are derived from a probability sample which initially contained approximately 9,200 manufacturing establishments and was drawn as a sub-sample from the 1974 Annual Survey of Manufactures (ASM). The ASM is a probability sample of approximately 70,000 establishments selected from the 1972 Census universe of over 300,000 plants and supplemented by samples of new manufacturing plants that began operations in 1973 and 1974. All major industry groups were represented in the capacity survey sample.

With a fixed sample size of 9,200 establishments, the use of a probability-proportionate-to-size sample design led to a certainty cutoff of about 2,000 employees. All in-scope establishments with employment of 2,000 or more were included in the sample with certainty. (The ASM sample panel includes all manufacturing establishments with 250 employees or more.) Smaller establishments were assigned subsampling probabilities so that their final probabilities of selection were proportional to employment, down to a minimum final probability of selection of .005. These establishments were arrayed by descending ASM-weighted employment within each 4-digit industry, and were sampled systematically. This sample design led to a survey panel of about 900 certainty establishments and approximately 8,300 noncertainty establishments.

The estimated utilization rates and proportions shown in this report were computed as employment-weighted utilization rates and proportions. These estimates were computed as

$$\hat{R} = \frac{{}_h \Sigma W_h TE_h Y_h a_h}{{}_h \Sigma W_h TE_h a_h}$$

where, for the hth selected establishment:

W_h is the sample weight,

TE_h is the total employment,

Y_h is the utilization rate or reported value for the estimate

a_h = 1 if the establishment h was selected in the sample and 0 if the establishment h was not selected.

Estimates of the variances were computed as:

$$\hat{V}(\hat{R}) = \frac{{}_h \Sigma W_h (W_h - 1) TE^2_h Y^2_h a_h}{(\Sigma W_h TE_h a_h)^2}$$

As not all of the original panel were operational in 1976, only about 8,300 manufacturing plants were mailed a questionnaire. Seven thousand three hundred plants or about 88 percent returned a report form which contained usable data.

The utilization rate estimates are based entirely on the response data. No attempt was made to impute data for individual nonrespondents; however, in the tabulation of the U.S. and durable-nondurable utilization rates, a check was made to see that differing response rates for major industry groups did not affect these higher level totals. It was found that differing response rates did not affect the higher level totals.

Table C-1 presents mailing and reporting rates by major industry group, with a breakdown for certainty cases, while table C-2 shows the response rate for each item on the report form.

Table C-1.--NUMBER OF REPORTS MAILED AND NUMBER OF USABLE REPORTS RECEIVED, BY MAJOR INDUSTRY GROUP, FOR THE 4th QUARTER 1976

Major industry group[1]	Number of reports mailed	Number of usable reports received[2]	Percent usable	Number of certainty reports mailed	Number of usable certainty reports[2]	Percent usable
UNITED STATES, TOTAL..........	8,291	7,315	88	862	806	94
Nondurable (20-23, 26-31)...........	3,668	3,185	87	208	185	89
Food and kindred products (20)........	852	712	84	28	24	86
Tobacco manufactures (21)........	22	22	100	7	7	100
Textile mill products (22)........	454	393	87	22	22	100
Apparel and other textile products (23)........	646	510	79	14	11	79
Paper and allied products (26)........	319	297	93	12	10	83
Printing and publishing (27)........	491	430	88	33	26	79
Chemicals and allied products (28)........	379	356	94	54	51	94
Petroleum and coal products (29)........	67	66	99	8	7	88
Rubber and plastics products, n.e.c. (30)........	315	292	93	27	26	96
Leather and leather products (31)........	123	107	87	3	1	33
Durable (24, 25, 32-39)...........	4,623	4,130	89	654	621	95
Lumber and wood products (24)........	341	283	83	2	1	50
Furniture and fixtures (25)........	238	204	86	10	7	70
Stone, clay, and glass products (32)........	316	277	88	11	10	91
Primary metal industries (33)........	460	429	93	99	95	96
Fabricated metal products (34)........	721	659	91	52	50	96
Machinery, except electrical (35)........	899	807	90	108	103	95
Electrical equipment and supplies (36)........	704	644	91	146	136	93
Transportation equipment (37)........	516	468	91	188	187	99
Instruments and related products (38)........	202	183	91	26	26	100
Miscellaneous manufacturing industries (39)........	226	176	78	12	6	50

N.e.c. Not elsewhere classified.

[1]Based on the 1972 Standard Industrial Classification system.
[2]Usable report is defined as one which contained at least the 1976 practical capacity utilization rate.

Table C-2.—RESPONSES BY ITEM ON SURVEY OF PLANT CAPACITY, 4th QUARTER 1976

(Number of establishments reporting)

Item	Actual operations	Preferred capacity	Practical capacity
1. Shifts per day....................	7,312	7,317	7,317
2. Days per week in operation........	7,312	7,317	7,314
3. Hours per days in operation.......	7,312	7,317	7,317
4. Number of production workers......	7,311	7,315	7,315
5. Total man-hours....................	7,311	7,314	7,311
6. Percent of overtime hours.........	5,695	3,801	4,239
7. Value of production...............	6,994	6,943	6,930
8. Quantity of production............	4,103	4,015	4,023
9. Quantity of materials consumed....	2,439	2,365	2,371

Number of reporters of:

10. 1976 preferred rate...............			7,315
11. 1976 practical rate...............			7,315
12. Reasons for operation at less than capacity......			6,692
13. Length of time to reach practical capacity.......			6,270
14. Length of time practical capacity could be maintained.......			6,430

Note: See appendix A for a more complete explanation of the questions.

All respondents were not required to answer each question. For instance, of the 7,315 reporters of 1976 practical rate, only 6,270 reported on how long it would take to reach that level (assuming sufficient demand). As many plants were at 100 percent capacity already, they were not required to answer that question.

Appendix C

Statistics of Shift Work and Plant Hours in U.S. Manufacturing

Because the figures are not generally familiar, a brief discussion of some of the Census Bureau and other data related to shift operations in U.S. manufacturing is appropriate. Information for 1929 appears in appendix D.

Census Surveys of Plant Capacity

Quoted below from the 1976 survey are Census Bureau instructions to survey respondents that are pertinent to the data on shifts and hours worked by plants:

> Shifts Per Day—Most shifts are assumed to be of 8 hours duration so that a 3-shift operation is usually maximum. If you are operating with a variation that leads to more than three shifts or to fractional shifts, please use the remarks to explain briefly your operations.
>
> Days Per Week and Hours Per Day—Refer to the duration the plant is open and operating, not the man-hours put in by your work force. . . .
>
> In reporting shifts, days, and hours of operations you may use the most typical pattern during the period.[1]

Although Census Bureau forms refer to fractional shifts, neither the forms used in the 1970s (nor the 1929 Census of Manufactures) define fractional shifts or provide instructions for their reporting. A plant with three departments, two of which operated a single eight-hour shift and one of which operated two eight-hour shifts could be thought of as operating fractional shifts. Under these circumstances, weights for combining departments working different hours in prin-

[1] U.S. Department of Commerce, Bureau of the Census, *Survey of Plant Capacity Fourth Quarter 1976*, MQ-C1.

ciple should reflect fixed assets valued in constant dollars. In field pretests Census Bureau statisticians found that plants used a variety of methods to combine departments when plant hours varied from department to department; however, only a small proportion of respondents report fractional shifts.

The Census Bureau is now engaged in a review of its current methodology for computing number of shifts, plant hours operated per day, and plant days operated per week. That review had not been completed in time for the revised 1978 publication schedule for release in early 1981. In the opinion of census statisticians the effect of this review on levels of the relevant measures is not expected to be large.

Bureau of Labor Statistics Data on Employment by Shift

The Bureau of Labor Statistics (BLS) has two long-established surveys in which some shift information is collected. For several years the BLS, through its Area Wage Surveys, has been publishing information on production worker employment on first, second, and third shifts in manufacturing plants in metropolitan areas. The Area Wage Surveys were initiated in the late 1940s but were not fully developed until 1960. Since then the BLS has published survey results annually. Related data on employment by shift appear in Industry Wage Surveys, but these, which focus on detailed industries, were not designed as continuous time series, and the results have not been aggregated.

There is some interest in levels of plant hours or shifts, although this study is mainly concerned with long-run change. The two data sources that invite comparison of levels because they are both up-to-date—the census and the BLS—are not easy to compare. Aside from locational differences, there are plant-size differences; the BLS Area Wage Surveys exclude small plants, which use multiple shifts less than large plants do. The possible bias on this account must be small, given the heavy concentration of employment in large plants. Aside from a few large standard metropolitan statistical areas, the BLS surveys a given standard metropolitan statistical area only once in three years. For example, the BLS figures for 1976 reflect employment in three years with weights approximately as follows: 1974 (1/3), 1975 (1/2), and 1976 (1/6).

The table below shows the percent distribution of production worker employment in manufacturing, by shift, according to the BLS Area Wage Survey of 1976.[2] Note that employment on the first shift

---

[2] U.S. Department of Labor, Bureau of Labor Statistics, *Area Wage Statistics: Metropolitan Areas, United States and Regional Summaries*, Bulletin 1900-82 (August 1979).

includes first-shift employment in two- and three-shift plants.

On first shift	73.2
On second shift	19.2
On third shift	7.6
Total	100.0
Average number of shifts	1.37

Clearly shifts are not equal in terms of employment. Comprehensive information on output or capital input by shift does not exist, textiles being an important exception.[3] Making certain assumptions about capital, one can make some inferences about plant operations using the BLS data shown above. Suppose that capital use is assumed to be proportional to employment by shift and 73.2 is taken to represent total available capital. The capital that runs three shifts is 7.6. The capital that runs two shifts but not more is 19.2 − 7.6 = 11.6, and the capital that runs only one shift is 73.2 − 11.6 − 7.6 or 54.0. Using these figures as weights yields an average number of shifts equal to 1.37.[4] This figure is far below the figure of 1.9 given in table 1 for 1976. The data showing the distribution of employment by shift must be used with great care if they are not to give a misleading view of plant operations. It is possible to cite many examples of around-the-clock or three-shift industries in which most workers are employed on the first shift or in which workers on second and third shifts are much less than the two-thirds that might be expected if employment by shift were equal. The industries below are known to be continuous or to have a heavy concentration of three-shift operations. The employment percentages are from BLS studies:

Industry	Date of Survey	Percent of Workers on Late Shifts
Petroleum refining	March–April 1966	32.1
Industrial chemicals	November 1965	35.1
Synthetic fibers	February–April 1966	45.8
Paper, pulp, and board	October 1967	46.5
Basic iron and steel	September 1967	47.8
Synthetic textiles	September 1965	42.7
Cotton textiles	July–August 1965	53.4

[3] See Foss, "The Utilization of Capital Equipment," *Survey of Current Business*, vol. 43, no. 6 (June 1963), p. 16.

[4] See Paul Taubman and Peter Gottschalk, "The Average Workweek of Capital in Manufacturing," *Journal of the American Statistical Association*, vol. 66, no. 335 (September 1971), pp. 448-55. Also Foss, "The Utilization of Capital Equipment," p. 16.

Investigators of foreign economies have found the same sort of differences in measures of shift operations. The table below, based on samples of plants, is taken from Betancourt and Clague.[5] The first column is an unweighted mean number of shifts per factory similar to the kind of figure that the Census Bureau is now publishing. The second column is a mean number of shifts, weighted by the factory fixed capital stock. In the third column, the total number of production workers is divided by production workers on the first shift. Note that it is typically well below the value in the first column.

	(1)	(2)	(3)
France	1.65	1.95	1.23
Japan	1.51	2.26	1.16
Israel	2.34	2.80	1.40
India	2.28	2.79	2.00
Yugoslavia	2.77	2.93	1.59

A new BLS survey that focuses on the time of day of employment was instituted in May 1973 and first published in 1978 with data for May 1977. It is based on the Current Population Survey rather than on a canvas of establishments. Results for May 1977, covering full-time wage and salary workers, show 80 percent of such employees in manufacturing on the daytime shift and a somewhat smaller proportion if only "operatives" other than truck drivers are considered. These results (see table 28) are broadly similar to those collected in the Area Wage Surveys and Industry Wage Surveys. It is interesting that in public utilities, in which capital operates on a twenty-four-hour per day basis, 88 percent of the workers work the daytime shift.

The important thing for this particular study is that it puts its main emphasis on long-term change in which comparisons over time are based on data obtained from very similar sets of questions.

---

[5] Roger R. Betancourt and Christopher K. Clague, "Multiple Shifts and the Employment Problem in Less-Developed Countries," *International Labor Review*, vol. 114, no. 2 (September-October 1976), pp. 187-96.

TABLE 28

Number and Percentage Distribution of Nonfarm Wage and Salary Workers Who Usually Work Full Time, by Shift and Industry, May 1977

Industry Division and Group	Number (thousands)					Percent				
	Total	Day	Evening	Night	Other	Total	Day	Evening	Night	Other
Total	58,975	49,382	4,871	2,021	2,700	100	84	8	3	5
Goods-producing[a]	21,774	17,952	2,218	991	613	100	82	10	5	3
Mining	631	484	82	45	20	100	77	13	7	3
Construction	3,727	3,544	41	9	133	100	95	1	—	4
Manufacturing	17,210	13,740	2,094	937	439	100	80	12	5	3
Durable goods	10,240	8,272	1,301	461	206	100	81	13	5	2
Lumber and wood	506	406	64	14	22	100	80	13	3	4
Stone, clay, glass	511	402	52	37	20	100	79	10	7	4
Primary metal	1,062	721	192	127	22	100	68	18	12	2
Fabricated metal	1,276	1,047	167	46	17	100	82	13	4	1
Machinery, except electrical	1,977	1,689	186	61	41	100	86	9	3	2
Electrical equipment and supplies	1,726	1,465	179	58	24	100	85	10	3	1
Transportation equipment	1,778	1,309	349	87	34	100	74	20	5	2
Other	1,403	1,232	112	32	28	100	88	8	2	2

Nondurable goods	6,970	5,468	793	476	233	100	79	11	7	3
Food	1,467	1,153	141	89	84	100	79	10	6	6
Textiles	864	530	178	132	23	100	61	21	15	3
Apparel	1,051	995	20	6	30	100	95	2	1	3
Paper	575	399	97	51	28	100	70	17	9	5
Printing and publishing	898	724	109	47	18	100	81	12	5	2
Chemicals	1,006	807	107	55	37	100	80	11	6	4
Rubber and plastics	584	402	101	76	4	100	69	17	13	1
Other	526	457	39	21	8	100	87	7	4	2
Service-producing	37,201	31,430	2,654	1,030	2,087	100	85	7	3	6
Transportation	2,166	1,531	284	152	199	100	71	13	7	9
Public utilities	2,057	1,801	124	55	77	100	88	6	3	4
Wholesale trade	2,945	2,693	46	36	170	100	91	2	1	6
Retail trade	7,263	5,857	822	128	455	100	81	11	2	6
Except eating and drinking places	5,858	5,082	369	84	323	100	87	6	1	6
Eating and drinking places	1,405	775	453	44	133	100	55	32	3	9
Banking and finance	1,601	1,514	38	20	29	100	95	2	1	2
Insurance and real estate	1,959	1,805	27	15	111	100	92	1	1	6
Services[b]	15,025	12,822	970	445	788	100	85	6	3	5
Business	1,169	976	90	54	50	100	83	8	5	4
Repair	598	553	15	2	28	100	93	3	—	5
Personal, except household	961	774	109	26	53	100	81	11	3	6
Private household	293	236	9	8	41	100	81	3	3	14
Entertainment and recreation	393	277	55	5	55	100	71	14	1	14

(Table continues)

TABLE 28 (continued)

Industry Division and Group	Number (thousands)					Percent				
	Total	Day	Evening	Night	Other	Total	Day	Evening	Night	Other
Professional	11,529	9,931	689	350	558	100	86	6	3	5
Hospital	2,558	1,889	360	245	65	100	74	14	10	3
Other^c	8,971	8,042	329	105	493	100	90	4	1	5
Public administration	4,185	3,407	342	179	257	100	81	8	4	6
Federal except postal	1,386	1,266	58	21	42	100	91	4	2	3
Postal	571	429	55	73	14	100	75	10	13	3
State	746	661	49	19	17	100	89	7	3	2
Local	1,482	1,051	181	67	184	100	71	12	5	12

NOTE: Because of rounding, detail may not equal totals.

a Includes agriculture.

b Includes forestry and fisheries, not shown separately.

c Includes welfare, religious, educational, and medical except hospital services.

SOURCE: U.S. Department of Labor, "6.9 Million Workers on Late Shifts," Press Release 78-188, March 16, 1978.

Appendix D

Obtaining Manufacturing Data for 1929

For this project the Census Bureau selected a probability sample of approximately 9,000 establishments from the 1929 Census of Manufactures. The 9,000 establishments were taken from a microfilm file of the individual returns, which was virtually complete. Returns in the file were grouped by detailed industry and, within each industry, by state. All establishments with more than 500 wage earners were taken with certainty. There were approximately 2,700 establishments of this size, and they accounted for 37.8 percent of monthly average wage earner employment in 1929. For the noncertainty part, plants were chosen in proportion to their importance in wage earner employment for *all manufacturing combined*. This resulted in the following samples and sampling ratios with respect to employment size.

Wage Earner Employment Size	Establishments in Sample	Sampling Ratio
1– 5	255	1 in 308
6– 20	752	1 in 75
21– 50	1,021	1 in 26
51–100	1,098	1 in 12
101–250	1,987	1 in 5
251–500	1,254	1 in 3
501 and over	2,659	1 in 1
Total	9,026	

After the sample was chosen, the Census Bureau discovered that six detailed industries had apparently not been microfilmed and are presumably lost. In addition, one reel of microfilm, containing five industries, could not be found. These eleven industries account for just 0.6 percent of wage earner employment (see table 29).

75

TABLE 29
EMPLOYMENT IN MISSING INDUSTRIES

1929 Industry Code	Industry Name	1929 Wage Earner Employment
110	Coffee and spices	9,053
125	Peanuts	7,933
222	Flax and hemp	47
302	Billiard and pool tables	1,390
1316	Windmills	1,554
1620	Instruments, professional and scientific	16,876
601	Alcohol	1,484
602	Ammunition	7,223
603	Baking powders	3,006
605	Bluing	105
607	Candles	781
Total in missing industries		49,452
All manufacturing		8,838,743
Missing as percent of all manufacturing		0.6

SOURCE: Census of Manufactures, 1929.

The Census Bureau decided to code *all* information on the 1929 schedule, which is reproduced below, except for questions 9a–9f, which provide detailed product information, and question 12, distribution of sales. Total value of products under question 9 was obtained. The questions pertaining to plant operations and shifts appear in item 4.

[Page 1 of Manufactures General Schedule]

CONFIDENTIAL GOVERNMENT REPORT

File No. ....

<table>
<tr><td>

FOR OFFICE USE ONLY

....
(State and County)

....
(City)

....
(Industry Number)

</td><td>

Form 100

DEPARTMENT OF COMMERCE

BUREAU OF THE CENSUS

WASHINGTON

</td><td>

The law makes it obligatory upon every manufacturer to furnish census data. All answers will be held in strict confidence.

</td></tr>
</table>

CENSUS OF MANUFACTURES, 1929

REQUIRED BY ACT OF CONGRESS APPROVED JUNE 18, 1929

GENERAL SCHEDULE

Under the law, no one not a sworn employee of the Bureau of the Census will be permitted to examine your report, and no information can or will be given out by the Bureau of the Census to any person outside that Bureau, whether in Government or in private life, which would disclose, exactly or approximately, any of the facts or figures in your report.

GENERAL INSTRUCTIONS.—Reports are required from all plants. Separate reports are required for plants in different counties and for those in different cities having 10,000 inhabitants or more. A combined report may be made for two or more plants in the same city or in the same county when located in places with fewer than 10,000 inhabitants. Name and location of each plant must be specified. Data for mining and quarrying should be omitted. (See accompanying instructions in regard to transportation and merchandising activities.)

1. **DESCRIPTION OF PLANT.**—*If this report covers more than one plant, give name and location of each, under "Remarks," page 4. (See "General Instructions," above.)*

    a. NAME OF PLANT ....

    b. NAME OF OWNER OR OPERATOR ....

    Is this owner or operator an incorporated concern? ....
    (Yes or No)

    LOCATION OF PLANT

    c. STATE ....   d. CITY, TOWN, OR VILLAGE ....

    e. COUNTY ....   f. STREET AND NUMBER ....

    g. POST OFFICE ADDRESS IF DIFFERENT FROM LOCATION (d) ....

    h. IS PLANT LOCATED WITHIN BOUNDARIES OF CITY, TOWN, OR VILLAGE AS INCORPORATED? .... If not, name the
    (Yes or No)
    township, borough, or other civil division in which the plant is located ....

    i. IS THIS A NEW PLANT WHICH STARTED OPERATIONS AFTER JANUARY 1, 1928? ....
    (Yes or No)

    j. INDICATE BY CHECK MARK (√) IN PROPER SPACE WHETHER, SINCE JANUARY 1, 1928, THIS PLANT HAS CHANGED ITS
    NAME ....; LOCATION ....; OWNERSHIP ....; GENERAL NATURE OF BUSINESS .... If so, give former name,
    location, ownership, or nature of business ....

    k. IS THIS PLANT A BRANCH OR SUBSIDIARY OF SOME OTHER CONCERN? .... If so, give name and address of
    (Yes or No)
    such concern ....

2. **CHARACTER OF INDUSTRY.**—These answers should be as definite as possible in brief space, indicating specific products and materials, not broad general classes. Return with the schedule a card, catalogue, or other printed matter ordinarily used by the concern to show the nature of its business.

    a. PRODUCTS ....
    (Specify chief kinds of goods manufactured or kinds of work done)

    b. MATERIALS USED ....
    (Specify principal kinds of materials or stock, in order of importance)

3. **PERIOD COVERED.**—This report should relate *preferably* to the calendar year 1929; but it may be made to cover the business or fiscal year ending within the period from April 1, 1929, to March 31, 1930. It should, in either case, cover a full year's operations, unless the plant was newly organized or went out of business within the year.

    The fiscal year or period covered by the information given below— { Began ...., 192....
    { Ended ...., 19....

4. **TIME IN OPERATION AND HOURS OF LABOR:**

    a. NUMBER OF DAYS THE PLANT WAS OPERATED DURING PERIOD COVERED ....
    (Give the number of days the plant, or any important part of it, was in operation. Days when shut down for repairs or for other causes should not be included. Do not include Sundays and holidays unless the plant was in actual operation.)

    (In answering b, c, and d, give figures based on practice followed during the year, without attempting to indicate minor variations; take note of e.)

    b. NORMAL NUMBER OF HOURS PLANT WAS OPERATED: PER DAY ....; PER WEEK ....

    c. NORMAL NUMBER OF SHIFTS PER DAY ....

    d. NORMAL NUMBER OF HOURS PER WEEK FOR THE INDIVIDUAL WAGE EARNER ....

    Does this number of hours refer to a 6-day, a 5½-day, or a 5-day week, or to some other basis (specify)? ....

    e. IF DURING PROLONGED PERIODS THE PLANT WORKED PART TIME (part of the normal working days per week or part of the normal hours per day), GIVE REASONS AND APPROXIMATE DATES ....

8—5546   (OVER)   11—8815

5. PERSONS ENGAGED.—Number December 14, 1929, as per pay roll. If this was not a representative day, give data for the nearest representative or normal day, stating here what date is used. Do not count the same person twice under different headings.

	MALE	FEMALE
a. PROPRIETOR OR FIRM MEMBERS (not applicable to incorporated companies)		
Salaried employees as follows:		
b. PRINCIPAL OFFICERS OF CORPORATIONS. (Do not include directors unless holding other offices on salary)		
c. MANAGERS, SUPERINTENDENTS, AND OTHER RESPONSIBLE ADMINISTRATIVE EMPLOYEES; FOREMEN AND OVERSEERS WHO DEVOTE ALL OR THE GREATER PART OF THEIR TIME TO SUPERVISORY DUTIES; CLERKS, STENOGRAPHERS, BOOKKEEPERS, AND OTHER CLERICAL EMPLOYEES ON SALARY. (Do not include foremen and overseers in minor positions; see 5-d.)		
Total salaried employees (sum of *b* and *c*)		
d. WAGE EARNERS.—(Report skilled and unskilled workers of all classes, including engineers, firemen, watchmen, packers, etc.; also foremen and overseers in minor positions who perform work similar to that done by the employees under their supervision. Include pieceworkers employed in the plant covered by this report, but do not include persons working in other plants or at home on materials furnished by your establishment.)		

6. WAGE EARNERS EMPLOYED, BY MONTHS.—Give number on pay roll for week which included 15th day of month, if this was a normal week. If not, give number for a normal week. (Follow instructions under Inquiry 3 as to who are to be included.) Figures given in this inquiry should relate to *calendar year 1929.* If remainder of report refers to some other period, give number "Remarks" (page 4) figures for those months in 1928 or 1930 which fall within that period. (See Inquiry 3.)

Jan. .... Feb. .... Mar. .... Apr. .... May.................... June....................

July .... Aug. .... Sept. .... Oct. .... Nov. .... Dec. ....

7. SALARIES AND WAGES.—Amounts paid during the period covered by this report. Include bonuses or percentages of profits when paid either to officers and salaried employees or to wage earners.

a. TOTAL AMOUNT OF SALARIES OF PRINCIPAL OFFICERS OF CORPORATIONS (see Inquiry 5–b) .... $....................

b. TOTAL AMOUNT OF SALARIES OF MANAGERS, SUPERINTENDENTS, AND OTHER RESPONSIBLE ADMINISTRATIVE EMPLOYEES; FOREMEN AND OVERSEERS; CLERKS, STENOGRAPHERS, BOOKKEEPERS, AND OTHER CLERICAL EMPLOYEES ON SALARY (see Inquiry 5–b) .... $....................

c. TOTAL AMOUNT PAID TO WAGE EARNERS, AS DEFINED UNDER INQUIRY 5–d .... $....................

Aggregate of salaries and wages (sum of items *a*, *b*, and *c*) .... $....................

8. MATERIALS, FUEL, AND ELECTRIC CURRENT.—The items entered below should relate *preferably* to the amounts of materials, fuel, and electric current *actually used* during the period covered; but if it is impracticable to report materials and fuel on this basis, enter the costs of the amounts purchased during the period. Include freight and haulage costs, but not the cost of haulage performed by the plant's own employees and equipment if practicable to segregate it. Place a check mark (√) after the word "used" or "purchased," as the case may be, in the space below.

The entries for materials and fuel, as given for this inquiry, refer to the costs of the amounts— Used.................... Purchased....................

a. COST OF ALL MATERIALS AND RAW STOCK ACTUALLY USED (including those transferred from other plants under the same ownership) during the period covered by this report, which entered into the products manufactured, together with the cost of containers for sale with products. *Do not include cost of mill or shop supplies* .... $....................

b. COST OF FUEL ACTUALLY USED (including that transferred from mines, wells, or plants under the same ownership) during the period covered by this report (total of items in Inquiry 11–a) .... $....................

c. COST OF PURCHASED ELECTRIC CURRENT (see Inquiry 11–b) .... $....................

Total cost of materials, fuel, and electric current (sum of *a*, *b*, and *c*) .... $....................

9. PRODUCTS.—Report the net selling values at the plant of all products of your own manufacture shipped or delivered to customers (or to warehouses on customers' accounts) during the period covered; or, if transferred to other plants under the same ownership, the value at which the transfers were made. All products, including by-products, should be covered. The principal products should be reported separately. Values should include those of containers sold with products. Report value at the factory (not at some other point of delivery).

PRODUCTS (report chief products separately)	QUANTITY	VALUE
a.		$....................
b.		$....................
c.		$....................
d. All other (specify)		$....................
		$....................
e. Contract work done in your plant on materials furnished by others (total receipts)		$....................
f. Custom work and repairing (total receipts)		$....................
Total value of products		$....................

If the value of the products actually *manufactured* during the period covered by this report *differed by more than 10 per cent* from that of the products *shipped or delivered*, give also, in the space indicated, the exact or estimated value, based on *selling prices f. o. b. factory*, of the products *manufactured* (including receipts for contract and custom work and repairing).

Value of products manufactured, $....................

1—5846   (2)   11—8815

10. POWER EQUIPMENT.—Give figures for equipment as of the end of the period covered by this report.

Important Note.—The form of this inquiry is different from that previously used, the purpose being to distinguish between active and inactive prime movers and generators. It is desired, at the same time, to obtain a total which shall be comparable with that reported at the 1927 census, when the inquiry called simply for a combined total of "all power equipment in the plant, active and emergency." By "emergency" equipment is meant that which is capable of being put into operation promptly, but which is used only in case of breakdown of the active equipment or at rather rare intervals when an exceptional load occurs. Equipment which is regularly used, but not usually on full time, should be classed as active.

	NUMBER	HORSEPOWER
a. PRIME MOVERS—total, active and emergency: Steam engines		
Steam turbines		
Internal-combustion engines (oil, gas, gasoline, etc.)		
Water wheels and turbines		
Total of above. Rated horsepower of above equipment which is not ordinarily active (included in "Total of above") _____ Horsepower	x x x x x	x x x x x x x
b. ELECTRIC MOTORS DRIVEN BY PURCHASED CURRENT—total, active and emergency		
c. ELECTRIC MOTORS DRIVEN BY CURRENT GENERATED IN PLANT—total, active and emergency		KILOWATTS
d. ELECTRIC GENERATORS DRIVEN BY PRIME MOVERS IN THE PLANT (do not include rotary converters or motor-generator sets)—total, active and emergency		
Rated capacity of generators which are not ordinarily active (included in "Total, active and emergency") _____ Kilowatts	x x x x x	x x x x x x x

11. FUEL AND ELECTRIC CURRENT:

a. FUEL USED (including that transferred from mines, wells, or plants under the same ownership) during the period covered by this report. Include fuel used for all purposes—for power, heat, and light, or as material for making gas, coke, etc.—but do not include oil or gas if none is used except for lighting.

	UNIT OF QUANTITY	QUANTITY	COST DELIVERED AT FACTORY
Coal, anthracite	Long ton		$
Coal, bituminous	Short ton		$
Coke	Short ton		$
Fuel oils (including crude oil and gas oils)	Gallon		$
Gasoline and kerosene	Gallon		$
Natural gas	M cu. ft.		$
Manufactured gas	M cu. ft.		$
Total cost			$

b. ELECTRIC CURRENT. (Report current generated or purchased during the year for all uses; but a plant which buys current for lighting *only* should not report it.)

	KILOWATT HOURS	COST
Generated in the plant		x x x x x x x
Purchased		$

12. DISTRIBUTION OF SALES.—Report below, in the proper spaces, the values (at f. o. b. factory prices) of goods shipped or delivered to customers (or to warehouses on customers' accounts) during the period covered. The total should be the same as the total given for Inquiry 9, Products. If exact figures are not available, give the best possible approximations.

	AMOUNT
a. SALES TO MANUFACTURERS AND INTERPLANT TRANSFERS	$
b. SALES TO RAILROADS, PUBLIC-UTILITY COMPANIES, AND CONTRACTORS	$
c. SALES THROUGH BRANCH HOUSES WHICH ARE CONDUCTED AS DISTINCT WHOLESALE MERCHANDISING ESTABLISHMENTS	$
d. SALES THROUGH MANUFACTURERS' AGENTS, BROKERS, AND COMMISSION HOUSES	$
e. SALES THROUGH WHOLESALERS AND JOBBERS (INCLUDING EXPORTING HOUSES)	$
f. SALES TO RETAILERS, INCLUDING RETAIL STORES OWNED BY MANUFACTURER	$
g. SALES TO HOTELS, RESTAURANTS, AND INSTITUTIONS	$
h. SALES TO HOME CONSUMERS (THROUGH FIELD AGENTS OR OTHERWISE)	$
i. SALES NOT DISTRIBUTED ABOVE (INDICATE CHANNELS THROUGH WHICH SOLD):	$
Total sales (same as total for Inquiry 9)	$

THIS IS TO CERTIFY that the information contained in this report is correct and complete to the best of my knowledge and belief, and covers the period from _____, 192___, to _____, 19_____

_____
(Signature and official title of person furnishing the information)

_____
(Signature of special agent)

_____
(Address)

9—5846   (3)   11—8815

NOTE: The schedule also contained a blank page to allow space for remarks.

Appendix E
Samples of Basic Data Tabulations

Tables 30 and 31 are samples of basic data tabulations for detailed industries in 1976 and 1929, respectively. All estimates are subject to sampling error, which may be very large when sample size is small. These and other qualifications are discussed in appendix B in the case of the 1976 statistics and are part of the detailed 1929 tabulations. Requests for more detail should be addressed to the author.

TABLE 30
SAMPLE OF 1976 TABULATIONS

Industry Code Number	Abbreviated Title	Per Day		Per Week	
		Shifts	Hours	Days	Hours[a]
20	Food and kindred products	—	—	—	—
201	Meat products	1.4	11.5	5.1	58.6
2011	Meat packing	1.3	10.8	5.2	56.2
2013	Sausages	1.5	12.9	5.0	64.5
2016	Poultry dressing	1.4	10.9	5.0	54.5
2017	Poultry and egg processing	2.1	17.5	4.9	85.8
202	Dairy products	1.7	14.4	5.3	76.3

NOTE: Aggregations based on employment weights.
[a] Hours per week = industry hours per day times industry days per week.
SOURCE: Bureau of the Census, *Survey of Plant Capacity, 1976*, Current Industrial Reports Series MQ-C1(76)-2, unpublished tabulations.

TABLE 31

Sample of 1929 Tabulations

Industry Code Number	Abbreviated Title	Per Day		Per Week	
		Shifts	Hours	Days[a]	Hours
Group 1	Food and kindred products	1.3	11.9	6.0	71.1
101	Beverages	1.1	9.8	6.0	58.4
102	Biscuits and crackers	1.0	8.0	5.6	47.8
	Bakery products, other	1.6	14.0	6.0	84.5
103	Butter	1.0	10.1	6.2	61.9
104	Canning (fish)	1.0	8.7	5.7	49.7
105	Canning (fruits and vegetables)	1.1	10.0	5.7	56.6
106	Cereal preparations	2.3	18.3	5.8	106.0
107	Cheese	1.0	8.8	6.5	56.8
109	Chocolate and cocoa	1.6	12.6	5.9	74.4
111	Condensed milk	1.0	9.2	6.7	61.3

Note: Aggregations based on employment weights.

[a] Industry weekly hours (unrounded) divided by industry daily hours (unrounded) = days per week.

Source: Bureau of the Census, unpublished data.

Appendix F

Industry Classification

Since the focus of this article is on change, one has to be sure that an industry today is reasonably comparable in what it produces to an industry or its counterpart in 1929. A growing economy such as that of the United States poses many problems in this regard. Some industries no longer exist, whereas others did not exist in earlier years. The industry classification system used in 1976 obviously differs from that used in 1929. In 1929 sixteen broad industry groups were recognized in manufacturing and, within each of these, several detailed classifications were made. Today twenty broad industry groups are recognized, each with a two-digit designation. These are further subdivided into three-digit and four-digit classifications.

This study makes use of two basic sets of comparisons. One is at a broad level, what might be called the two-digit level. These were used in the first part of the study and are shown in table 32. The other is at a detailed level. Sometimes this may involve a comparison of a four-digit industry today with its detailed counterpart in 1929. At other times detailed industries were combined into larger aggregates to bring about comparability. This was used in the regression analysis, and its results are shown in table 33.

For the broad classification, some groups could be handled very easily, such as railroad repair shops, which constituted one of the sixteen major groups in manufacturing in 1929 but are excluded now. With one or two important exceptions at the two-digit classification level, one can bring about a reasonable degree of comparability between 1929 and 1976 with some relatively small additions or subtractions. This may be seen below, for example, in the case of food and kindred products. For 1976 industry classifications are those used in 1972 and in the Census of Manufactures for that year. Tables similar to food are shown for each current two-digit industry.

The main difficulty was with what are now primary metals (SIC 33) and fabricated metals (SIC 34). In 1929 primary and fabricated metals were grouped together, and the main division was between iron and steel on the one hand and nonferrous metals on the other. Consequently, what is shown in this study as primary metals for 1929 and 1976 is a truncated version of the complete industry as now officially defined.

Table 33 shows industries comparable at the most detailed level, which were used for the regressions. In practice a few industries that were judged comparable had to be dropped from the regressions where statistics pertaining to independent variables were not available. Approximately half of the ninety-five or so detailed industries used for the regressions consisted of single four-digit industries in 1976 and single detailed industries in 1929. Average hours of industries that are combinations of detailed industries were derived by weighting detailed industry hours with employment weights.

TABLE 32
BROAD INDUSTRIES AND INDUSTRY GROUPS USED IN COMPARISONS

1972 Classification	1929 Classification
SIC 20—Food and kindred products	Group 1—Food and kindred products
minus industries 2026, 2037, and 2038	plus industries 601, 617, 620, 622, 623, and 625
	minus industry 125
equals 1972 food comparable with 1929	equals 1929 food comparable with 1972
SIC 21—Tobacco products minus industry 2141 equals 1972 tobacco comparable with 1929	Sum of detailed industries 1608 and 1647 equals 1929 tobacco comparable with 1972
SIC 22—Textile mill products	Sum of detailed industries 216, 217, 218, 220, 222, 225, 233, 234a, 234b, 234c, 234d, 235, 236, 238, 244, 249, 250, 251, 253, 201, 241, 248, 206, 207, and 212
equals 1972 textiles comparable with 1929	equals 1929 textiles comparable with 1972

(Table continues)

TABLE 32   (continued)

1972 Classification	1929 Classification
SIC 23—Apparel and other textile products	Sum of detailed industries 208, 209, 211, 213, 223, 224, 228, 243, 245, 210, 215, 226, 239, 203, 204, 205, 219, 221, 227, 231, 232, 240, 242, 246, 229, 230, and 1615
equals 1972 apparel comparable with 1929	equals 1929 apparel comparable with 1972
SIC 24—Lumber and wood products minus industries 2451 and 2492 equals 1972 lumber comparable with 1929	Sum of detailed industries 301, 303, 304, 306, 307, 310, 311, 313, 314, 318, 319, and 320 equals 1929 lumber comparable with 1972
SIC 25—Furniture and fixtures	Sum of detailed industries 309, 1624, and 1651
equals 1972 furniture comparable with 1929	equals 1929 furniture comparable with 1972
SIC 26—Paper and allied products	Group 4—Paper and allied products
equals 1972 paper comparable with 1929	equals 1929 paper comparable with 1972
SIC 27—Printing and publishing	Sum of detailed industries 504, 505, 507, 508, 509, 510, and 512
equals 1972 printing comparable with 1929	equals 1929 printing comparable with 1972
SIC 28—Chemicals and allied products minus industry 2822	Sum of detailed industries 602, 604, 605, 606, 608, 609, 610, 611, 612, 613, 614, 615, 616, 618, 619, 621, 624, 626, 627, 628, 629, 630, 631, 632, and 633
equals 1972 chemicals comparable with 1929	equals 1929 chemicals comparable with 1972

1972 Classification	1929 Classification
SIC 29—Petroleum and coal products minus industry 2951 equals 1972 petroleum comparable with 1929	Sum of detailed industries 702, 704, 705, and 1638 equals 1929 petroleum comparable with 1972
SIC 30—Rubber and miscellaneous plastic products minus industry 3079 equals 1972 rubber comparable with 1929	Sum of detailed industries 801, 802, and 803 equals 1929 rubber comparable with 1972
SIC 31—Leather and leather products equals 1972 leather comparable with 1929	Sum of detailed industries 902, 903, 904, 905, 906, 907, 908, 909, 910, and 1622 equals 1929 leather comparable with 1972
SIC 32—Stone, clay, and glass products minus industry 3273 equals 1972 stone comparable with 1929	Group 10—Stone, clay, and glass products plus industries 1639 and 1644 equals 1929 stone comparable with 1972
SIC 33—Primary metal industries Sum of detailed industries 3312, 3317, 3331, 3332, 3333, 334, 335, and 336 equals 1972 primary metals comparable with 1929	Sum of detailed industries 701, 1110, 1112, 1113, 1128, 1126, 1201, 1215, 1216, 1217, 1218, and 1220 equals 1929 primary metals comparable with 1972
SIC 34—Fabricated metal products minus industries 3482, 3483, and 3489 equals 1972 fabricated metals comparable with 1929	Sum of detailed industries 1101, 1103, 1104, 1105, 1106, 1108, 1109, 1114, 1115, 1116, 1117, 1118, 1120, 1122, 1123, 1125, 1127, 1204, 1205, 1209, 1212, and 1219 equals 1929 fabricated metals comparable with 1972
SIC 35—Machinery, except electrical equals 1972 machinery comparable with 1929	Sum of detailed industries 1301, 1302, 1304, 1305, 1307, 1309, 1313, 1314, 1316, 1318, 502, 511, 513, 1610, 1641, and 316 equals 1929 machinery comparable with 1972

(Table continues)

TABLE 32 (continued)

1972 Classification	1929 Classification
SIC 36—Electric and electronic equipment	Sum of detailed industries 1303, 1310, 1312, 1315, 1207, and 1635
equals 1972 electrical machinery comparable with 1929	equals 1929 electrical machinery comparable with 1972
SIC 37—Transportation equipment minus industries 376 and 379	Sum of detailed industries 1401, 1405, 1406, 1407, 1408, 1409, and 1410
equals 1972 transportation equipment comparable with 1929	equals 1929 transportation equipment comparable with 1972
SIC 38—Instruments and related products	Sum of detailed industries 1620, 1311, 1119, 1306, 1631, 1645, 1611, 1636, 1221, 1223, 1222, and 1202
equals 1972 instruments comparable with 1929	equals 1929 instruments comparable with 1972
SIC 39—Miscellaneous manufacturing industries	Sum of detailed industries 1210, 1211, 1213, 1214, 1603, 1604, 1605, 1606, 1607, 1609, 1612, 1613, 1618, 1622, 1623, 1627, 1628, 1629, 1630, 1633, 1634, 1640, 1642, 1648, 1403, 305, 202, and 237
equals 1972 miscellaneous comparable with 1929	equals 1929 miscellaneous comparable with 1972

NOTE: n.e.c. = not elsewhere classified. Description of industry code numbers in 1929 may be found in U.S. Bureau of the Census, *Fifteenth Census of the United States, Manufactures: 1929*, vol. 1, pp. 336-345. Description of industry code numbers in 1972 may be found in U.S. Bureau of the Census, *Census of Manufactures, 1972, General Summary*, MC 72(1)-1, appendix B.
SOURCE: Author.

TABLE 33

Detailed Industries and Industry Groups Used in Regressions

Computer Code Number	1972 Industry	1929 Industry	1929 Designation (abbreviated)
1	2022	107	cheese
2	2023	111	condensed milk
3	2046	113	corn syrup
5	2062	131	sugar refining, cane
6	2066	109	chocolate
7	2086	101	beverages
8	2091	104	canning and preserving: fish
10	2098	121	macaroni
11	2065	112	confectionery
12	2075	623	oil, linseed
	2076	625	oil, n.e.c.
	2077		
13	2011	123	meat packing
	2013	128	sausage
14	2032	105	canning and preserving:
	2033		fruits and vegetables,
	2034		preserves
	2035		
	2037		
	2038		
15	2052	102a	biscuits and crackers
16	211	1608b	cigarettes
	212	1608a	cigars
17	2211	216	cotton goods
	2221	244	silk and rayon
	2296		
	228		
18	2251	234a	hosiery (knit goods)
	2252		

(Table continues)

TABLE 33   (continued)

Computer Code Number	1972 Industry	1929 Industry	1929 Designation (abbreviated)
19	2291	220	felt goods
20	2298	214	cordage and twine
21	2253	234b	underwear (knit goods)
			outerwear (knit goods)
			knit cloth (knit goods)
	2254	234c	
	2257	234d	
	2258		
	2259		
22	231	208	clothing, men's, etc., n.e.c.
	232	211	clothing, work, men's
		209	artificial leather
		213	collars, men's
		223	furnishing goods
		243	shirts
23	233	210	clothing, women's, n.e.c.
	234	215	corsets and allied garments
	236		
24	235	228	hats and caps, men's
		229	hats, fur, felt
		230	hats, wool, felt
		239	millinery
		1619	hats, straw, men's
25	2381	224	gloves and mittens
26	2391	232	house furnishing goods, n.e.c.
	2392		
27	2393	204	bags
28	2394	203	awnings, tents
29	241	311	lumber and lumber products
	242	314	planning mill products
	243	308	excelsior
		320	wood, turned and shaped
		318	windows and door screens
30	2491	317	turpentine and rosin

Computer Code Number	1972 Industry	1929 Industry	1929 Designation (abbreviated)
31	251	309	furniture
	252	1624	mattresses
	253	1651	window shades and fixtures
	254		
	259		
32	2611	410	pulp
33	2642	405	envelopes
34	271	510	printing and publishing,
	272		newspapers and periodicals
35	273	504	engraving, steel
	274	505	engraving, wood
	275	506	lithographing
	276	507	photoengraving
	277	508	printing and publishing, book and job
	2791	509	printing and publishing, music
	2793		
	2795		
36	278	501	bookbinding
37	2813	610	compressed gases
38	2841	604	blacking
	2842	609	cleaning preparations
		651	soap
39	2844	628	perfumes
40	2851	626	paints and varnishes
41	2873	614	fertilizers
	2874		
	2875		
42	2893	618	ink, printing
43	2992	704	lubricating oils
44	2952	1638	roofing
45	3011	803	rubber tires
46	3021	810	boots and shoes, rubber
47	3069	802	rubber goods
	3041		
	3031		*(Table continues)*

TABLE 33   (continued)

Computer Code Number	1972 Industry	1929 Industry	1929 Designation (abbreviated)
48	311	907	leather, tanned
49	313	902	boot and shoe cutstock
		903	boot and shoe findings
50	314	904	boot and shoes, not rubber
51	315	905	gloves and mittens, leather
52	316	910	trunks, suitcases
53	317	1622	jewelry cases
		908	pocketbooks
		906	leathers, n.e.c.
54	321	1008	glass
	322		
55	323	1016	mirrors
		1009	glass products
56	325	1004	clay products
	3297	1006	crucibles
57	326	1017	pottery
		1003	china
58	328	1014	marble
59	3317	1128	wrought pipe
60	3411	1123	tin cans and tinware
61	3412	1120	steel barrels
62	3421	1103	cutlery
	3423	1105	files
		1125	tools
63	3425	1116	saws
64	3429	1109	hardware, n.e.c.
65	3441	1122	structural steel
	3449		
66	3442	1104	door shutters, metals
67	3444	1204	copper, sheets iron work

Computer Code Number	1972 Industry	1929 Industry	1929 Designation (abbreviated)
68	345	1117	screw machine products
		1101	bolts, nuts, washers
69	3471	1205	electroplating
70	3484	1106	firearms
71	3495	1127	wirework, n.e.c.
	3496		
72	3541	1307	machine tools
	3542		
73	3544	1318	machine tool accessories
	3545	1625	models and patterns
74	3552	1313	textile machinery
75	3561	1309	pumps
	3586		
76	3633	1315	washing machines
77	3636	1312	sewing machines
78	3645	1207	gas and electric fixtures
	3646		
	3647		
	3648		
79	361	1303	electrical machinery
	362	1635	phonographs
	3631		
	3634		
	3639		
	3641		
	3643		
	3644		
	365		
	366		
	367		
	369		
80	371	1407	motor vehicle bodies and parts
		1408	motor vehicles
81	372	1401	aircraft
82	373	1410	ship and boat building

(Table continues)

TABLE 33   (continued)

Computer Code Number	1972 Industry	1929 Industry	1929 Designation (abbreviated)
83	374	1405	cars, railroad
		1406	locomotives
84	375	1409	motorcycles, bicycles
85	3832	1631	optical goods
	3851		
86	3843	1611	dental goods
87	3861	1636	photographic apparatus
88	3873	1221	watch materials
		1223	watch movements
		1222	watchcases
		1202	clocks
89	3914	1214	silversmithing
		1213	plated ware
90	3931	1627	musical instrument parts, piano
		1628	musical instrument parts, n.e.c.
		1629	musical instruments: organs
		1630	musical instruments: pianos
91	3942	1648	toys
	3944	1642	sporting goods
	3949	1403	carriages, children's
92	3951	1633	pencils, lead
	3952	1603	artists' materials
		1634	pens
93	3964	1612	fancy articles
		1609	combs
		1211	needles, pins
94	3991	1604	brooms
		1605	brushes
95	3993	1640	signs

NOTE: n.e.c. = not elsewhere classified.
SOURCE: See table 32.

Appendix G

Regional Distribution of Shift Work

Table 34 shows the distribution of employment according to the number of work shifts in major industries and in regions in 1976. Table 35 shows the same information for 1929 with 1929 industry classifications.

TABLE 34

PERCENTAGE DISTRIBUTION OF EMPLOYMENT BY NUMBER OF SHIFTS,
MAJOR INDUSTRY AND REGION, 1976

Industry and Region	Total Shifts	Under 2 Shifts	2–2.9 Shifts	3 or More Shifts
Food				
Northeast	100	46	28	26
North-central	100	43	33	24
South	100	62	26	12
West	100	52	23	25
Tobacco				
Northeast	100	71	—	29
North-central	100	—	—	—
South	100	13	34	54
West	100	—	—	—
Textiles				
Northeast	100	36	28	36
North-central	100	7	54	39
South	100	9	12	79
West	100	34	28	38

(Table continues)

TABLE 34 (continued)

Industry and Region	Total Shifts	Under 2 Shifts	2–2.9 Shifts	3 or More Shifts
Apparel				
Northeast	100	96	3	2
North-central	100	63	36	1
South	100	96	2	2
West	100	96	4	—
Lumber				
Northeast	100	85	15	—
North-central	100	82	10	8
South	100	78	16	6
West	100	54	31	16
Furniture and fixtures				
Northeast	100	88	12	—
North-central	100	59	34	6
South	100	85	15	—
West	100	85	15	—
Paper and allied products				
Northeast	100	23	25	52
North-central	100	12	30	58
South	100	9	21	70
West	100	22	15	63
Printing and publishing				
Northeast	100	46	33	21
North-central	100	44	29	27
South	100	44	30	27
West	100	47	32	21
Chemicals and allied products				
Northeast	100	29	22	49
North-central	100	42	22	36
South	100	12	6	82
West	100	29	29	42
Petroleum				
Northeast	100	38	17	45
North-central	100	31	—	69
South	100	—	—	100
West	100	4	—	96

Industry and Region	Total Shifts	Under 2 Shifts	2–2.9 Shifts	3 or More Shifts
Rubber and plastic				
Northeast	100	26	16	57
North-central	100	17	19	64
South	100	16	18	66
West	100	21	17	62
Leather				
Northeast	100	92	8	—
North-central	100	89	6	5
South	100	96	4	—
West	100	82	—	18
Stone, clay, and glass				
Northeast	100	32	16	53
North-central	100	46	13	41
South	100	41	19	40
West	100	38	18	44
Primary metal industries				
Northeast	100	14	28	58
North-central	100	16	23	62
South	100	16	18	66
West	100	7	13	80
Fabricated metal products				
Northeast	100	49	36	14
North-central	100	36	45	18
South	100	53	33	14
West	100	55	27	19
Machinery				
Northeast	100	45	33	22
North-central	100	37	39	24
South	100	44	37	19
West	100	53	27	19
Electrical and electronic equipment				
Northeast	100	55	26	20
North-central	100	55	24	20
South	100	48	36	16
West	100	48	35	16
Transportation equipment				
Northeast	100	36	38	26
North-central	100	31	53	16
South	100	38	45	18
West	100	37	48	15

(Table continues)

TABLE 34 (continued)

Industry and Region	Total Shifts	Under 2 Shifts	2–2.9 Shifts	3 or More Shifts
Instruments				
Northeast	100	57	34	9
North-central	100	51	41	8
South	100	49	32	19
West	100	81	16	3
Miscellaneous				
Northeast	100	76	16	9
North-central	100	63	22	15
South	100	81	9	10
West	100	73	23	4

SOURCE: U.S. Bureau of the Census, unpublished data.

TABLE 35
PERCENTAGE DISTRIBUTION OF EMPLOYMENT BY NUMBER OF SHIFTS, MAJOR INDUSTRY AND REGION, 1929

Industry and Region	Total Shifts	Under 2 Shifts	2–2.9 Shifts	3 or More Shifts
Food				
Northeast	100	69	22	9
North-central	100	80	11	9
South	100	65	28	7
West	100	80	8	11
Textiles and apparel				
Northeast	100	88	11	1
North-central	100	98	2	—
South	100	65	34	a
West	100	87	11	2
Forest products				
Northeast	100	99	1	a
North-central	100	95	5	—
South	100	94	6	—
West	100	75	25	a
Paper and allied products				
Northeast	100	46	12	41
North-central	100	55	8	36
South	100	52	25	23
West	100	22	—	78

Industry and Region	Total Shifts	Under 2 Shifts	2–2.9 Shifts	3 or More Shifts
Printing and publishing				
Northeast	100	73	20	8
North-central	100	80	16	5
South	100	77	18	5
West	100	85	15	—
Chemicals				
Northeast	100	57	9	34
North-central	100	68	10	22
South	100	33	23	43
West	100	61	—	39
Petroleum and coal products				
Northeast	100	7	4	89
North-central	100	3	—	97
South	100	4	2	93
West	100	—	6	94
Rubber products				
Northeast	100	84	7	9
North-central	100	23	11	66
South	100	22	17	60
West	100	—	9	91
Leather				
Northeast	100	99	—	1
North-central	100	100	—	—
South	100	100	—	—
West	100	100	—	—
Stone, clay, and glass				
Northeast	100	72	4	24
North-central	100	66	8	26
South	100	63	15	22
West	100	68	4	28
Iron and steel				
Northeast	100	58	17	25
North-central	100	55	10	35
South	100	48	12	40
West	100	68	29	3
Nonferrous metals				
Northeast	100	76	17	6
North-central	100	83	11	6
South	100	60	10	31
West	100	44	3	53

(Table continues)

TABLE 35 (continued)

Industry and Region	Total Shifts	Under 2 Shifts	2–2.9 Shifts	3 or More Shifts
Machinery				
Northeast	100	95	5	[a]
North-central	100	91	9	—
South	100	83	10	7
West	100	91	7	2
Transport equipment (air, land, water)				
Northeast	100	92	6	2
North-central	100	76	23	1
South	100	74	26	—
West	100	58	42	—
Miscellaneous				
Northeast	100	97	1	2
North-central	100	99	1	[a]
South	100	99	1	—
West	100	97	2	—

[a] Less than 0.5 percent.
SOURCE: U.S. Bureau of the Census, unpublished data.

Bibliography

Abramovitz, Moses. *Resource and Output Trends in the United States since 1870.* National Bureau of Economic Research, Occasional Paper 42. New York, 1956.

———. "Economic Growth in the United States." *American Economic Review* 52: 762–82.

Abramovitz, Moses, and David, Paul A. "Reinterpreting Economic Growth: Parables and Realities." *Papers and Proceedings of the American Economic Association,* May 1973.

American Engineering Council. *The Twelve-Hour Shift in Industry.* New York: E. P. Dutton, 1922.

Betancourt, Roger R., and Clague, Christopher K. "An Economic Analysis of Capital Utilization." *Southern Economic Journal* 42: 69–78.

———. "An Econometric Analysis of Capital Utilization." *International Economic Review* 19, no. 1 (February 1978).

———. "Multiple Shifts and the Employment Problem in Less-Developed Countries." *International Labor Review* 114: 187–96.

———. "Working Capital and Shift-Work in Imperfect Capital Markets." Unpublished, April 1976.

Cartter, Allan. *Proceedings of Ninth Annual Meeting, Industrial Relations Research Association* (1956): 224–27.

Christensen, Laurits R., and Jorgenson, Dale W. "The Measurement of U.S. Real Capital Input." *Review of Income and Wealth,* series 15 (1969): 293–320.

———. "U.S. Real Product and Real Factor Input, 1929–1967." *Review of Income and Wealth,* series 16 (1970): 19–50.

————. "Measuring the Performance of the Private Sector of the U.S. Economy, 1929–1969." In *Measuring Economic and Social Performance*, edited by Milton Moss. New York: Columbia University Press for National Bureau of Economic Research, 1973.

Clague, Christopher K. "The Theory of Capital Utilization: Some Extensions." Unpublished, April 1975.

Coen, Robert M. "The Effect of Cash Flow on the Speed of Adjustment." In *Tax Incentives and Capital Spending*, edited by G. Fromm. Washington, D.C.: Brookings Institution, 1971.

Creamer, Daniel; Dobrovolsky, Sergei; and Borenstein, Israel. *Capital in Manufacturing and Mining: Its Formation and Financing*. Princeton, N.J.: Princeton University Press for National Bureau of Economic Research, 1960.

Dankert, Clyde E. "Shorter Hours and Multiple Shifts: A Future Pattern?" *Personnel* 36: 61–69.

Dankert, Clyde E.; Mann, Floyd C.; and Northrup, Herbert R., eds. *Hours of Work*. New York: Harper and Row, 1965.

Denison, Edward F. *The Sources of Economic Growth in the United States and the Alternatives before Us*. Committee for Economic Development, Supplementary Paper No. 13. New York, 1962.

————. *Why Growth Rates Differ*. Washington, D.C.: Brookings Institution, 1967.

————. *Accounting for United States Economic Growth 1929–1969*. Washington, D.C.: Brookings Institution, 1974.

————. "Some Major Issues in Productivity Analysis: An Examination of Estimates by Jorgenson and Griliches" and "Final Comments." *Survey of Current Business* 52 (May 1972), part II.

————. *Accounting for Slower Economic Growth*. Washington, D.C.: Brookings Institution, 1979.

Fabricant, Solomon. *Basic Facts on Productivity Change*. National Bureau of Economic Research, Occasional Paper 63. New York, 1959.

Fellner, William. *Trends and Cycles in Economic Activity*. New York: Henry Holt and Company, 1956.

Foss, Murray F. "The Utilization of Capital Equipment." *Survey of Current Business* 43: 8–16.

Freeman, Richard, and Medoff, James. "New Estimates of Private Sector Unionism in the United States." *Industrial and Labor Relations Review* 32, no. 2.

Georgescu-Roegen, Nicholas. "The Economics of Production." *American Economic Review* 60: 1–9.

Goldsmith, Raymond W. *The National Wealth of the United States in the Postwar Period.* Princeton, N.J.: Princeton University Press for the National Bureau of Economic Research, 1962.

Gollop, Frank M., and Jorgenson, Dale W. "U.S. Productivity Growth by Industry, 1947–73." In *New Developments in Productivity Measurement and Analysis*, John W. Kendrick and Beatrice N. Vaccara, eds. Chicago, Ill.: University of Chicago Press for National Bureau of Economic Research, 1980.

Grose, Lawrence; Rottenberg, Irving; and Wasson, Robert. "New Estimates of Fixed Business Capital in the United States, 1925–65." *Survey of Current Business* 46, no. 12 (December 1966): 34–40.

Heathfield, David F. "The Measurement of Capital Usage Using Electricity Consumption Data for the U.K." *Journal of the Royal Statistical Society*, A, 135, Part 2: 208–20.

Hedges, Janice N., and Sekscenski, Edward S. "Workers on Late Shifts in a Changing Economy." *Monthly Labor Review* 102: 14–22.

Hickman, Bert G. *Investment Demand and U.S. Economic Growth.* Washington, D.C.: Brookings Institution, 1965.

Jaszi, George; Wasson, Robert C.; and Grose, Lawrence. "Expansion of Fixed Business Capital in the United States." *Survey of Current Business* 42, no. 11 (November 1962): 9–18, 28.

Jorgenson, D. W., and Griliches, Z. "The Explanation of Productivity Change." *Review of Economic Studies* 34: 249–83.

————. "Issues in Growth Accounting: A Reply to Edward F. Denison" and "Final Reply." *Survey of Current Business* 52 (May 1972), part II.

Kendrick, John W. *Productivity Trends in the United States.* Princeton, N.J.: Princeton University Press for National Bureau of Economic Research, 1961.

————. *Postwar Productivity Trends in the United States, 1948–1969.* New York: Columbia University Press for National Bureau of Economic Research, 1973.

————. *The Formation and Stocks of Total Capital.* New York: Columbia University Press for National Bureau of Economic Research, 1976.

Kendrick, John W., and Grossman, Elliott S. *Productivity in the United States: Trends and Cycles.* Baltimore, Md.: Johns Hopkins University Press, 1980.

Kim, Young D., and Winston, Gordon C. "The Optimum Utilization of Capital Stock and the Level of Economic Development." *Economica* 41: 337–86.

Kuznets, Simon. *Capital in the American Economy: Its Formation and Financing.* Princeton, N.J.: Princeton University Press for the National Bureau of Economic Research, 1961.

Kuznets, Simon, ed. *Income and Wealth of the United States.* Cambridge: Bowes and Bowes, 1952.

Malcomson, James M. "Capacity Utilization, the User Cost of Capital and the Cost of Adjustment." *International Economic Review* 16: 352–61.

Marris, Robin. *The Economics of Capital Utilization.* Cambridge: Cambridge University Press, 1964.

Maurice, Marc. *Shiftwork.* Geneva: International Labor Office, 1975.

Moloney, John F. "Some Effects of the Federal Fair Labor Standards Act upon Southern Industry." *Southern Economic Journal* 9: 15–23.

Mueller, Fredrick W., and Nix, James C. "Premium Pay: An Analysis of Industrial Practices." *Monthly Labor Review,* August 1951: 148–51.

Musgrave, John. "Fixed Nonresidential Business and Residential Capital in the United States, 1925–75." *Survey of Current Business* 56, no. 4: 46–52.

Nadiri, M. Ishaq. "Some Approaches to the Theory and Measurement of Total Factor Productivity: A Survey." *Journal of Economic Literature* 8: 1137–77.

Northrup, Herbert R., and Brinberg, Herbert R. *Economics of the Work Week.* National Industrial Conference Board, Studies in Business Economics, no. 24. New York, 1950.

Nourse, Edwin G., and Associates. *America's Capacity to Produce.* Washington, D.C.: Brookings Institution, 1934.

O'Connor, Charles M. "Late-Shift Employment in Manufacturing Industries." *Monthly Labor Review* 93, no. 11: 37–42.

Rees, Albert. *The Economics of Work and Pay.* 2d ed. New York: Harper and Row, 1979.

―――. *New Measures of Wage-Earner Compensation in Manufacturing, 1914–57.* National Bureau of Economic Research, Occasional Paper 75. New York, 1960.

Schultze, Charles L. "Some Effects of Changes in Working Hours on Investment, Output, and Real Wages." Paper given at Business and

Economic Statistics Section, American Statistical Association Convention, September 1956.

Scitovsky, T. "A Note on Profit Maximization and Its Implications." *Review of Economic Studies* 11 (1943).

Sloane, P. J. "Economic Aspects of Shift and Night Work in Industrial Market Economies." *International Labor Review* 117, no. 2 (March/April 1978).

Solow, Robert M. "Technical Change and the Aggregate Production Function." *Review of Economics and Statistics*, August 1957: 312–20.

Taubman, Paul, and Gottschalk, Peter. "The Average Workweek of Capital in Manufacturing." *Journal of the American Statistical Association* 66: 448–55.

Taubman, Paul; Gottschalk, Peter; and Wilkinson, Maurice. "User Cost, Capital Utilization and Investment Theory." *International Economic Review* 11: 209–15.

Terleckyj, Nestor. "Factors Underlying Productivity: Some Empirical Observations." *Journal of the American Statistical Association* 53 (June 1958): 593.

———. "Sources of Productivity Change: A Pilot Study Based on the Experience of American Manufacturing Industries, 1948–1953." Ph.D. dissertation, Columbia University, 1959.

Ture, Norman B. *Accelerated Depreciation in the United States, 1954–60.* New York: Columbia University Press for the National Bureau of Economic Research, 1967.

U.S. Department of Commerce. Bureau of the Census. *Census of Manufactures, 1929.*

———. *Census of Manufactures, 1972.*

———. *Annual Survey of Manufactures, 1976.*

———. *Survey of Plant Capacity,* MQ-C1, 1973, 1974, 1975, 1976, 1977.

U.S. Department of Commerce. Bureau of Economic Analysis. "Fixed Nonresidential Business and Residential Capital in the United States, 1973–75." *Survey of Current Business* 56, no. 8: 64.

U.S. Department of Labor. Bureau of Labor Statistics. *Area Wage Statistics: Metropolitan Areas, United States and Regional Summaries.* Bulletin 1900–82 (August 1979).

———. *State Labor Laws for Women.* Bulletin of the Women's Bureau, no. 156, 1938.

————. "6.9 Million Workers on Late Shifts." USDL Press Release 78–188, March 16, 1978.

Winston, Gordon C. "Capital Utilization in Economic Development." *Economic Journal* 81: 36–60.

————. "Capital Utilization and Optimal Shift Work." *Bangladesh Economic Review* 11: 515–58.

————. "The Theory of Capital Utilization and Idleness." *Journal of Economic Literature* 12: 1301–20.

Winston, Gordon C., and McCoy, Thomas O. "Investment and the Optimal Idleness of Capital." *Review of Economic Studies* 41: 419–28.

Zalusky, John. "Shift Work—A Complex of Problems." *The AFL-CIO Federationist* 85: 1–6.

A Note on the Book

The typeface used for the text of this book is
Palatino, designed by Hermann Zapf.
The type was set by
Hendricks-Miller Typographic Company, Washington, D.C.
Everybodys Press, of Hanover, Pennsylvania, printed
and bound the book, using Warren's Olde Style paper.
The cover and format were designed by Pat Taylor.
The manuscript was edited by George Dorsey, and
by Donna Spitler of the AEI Publications staff.

SELECTED AEI PUBLICATIONS

The AEI Economist, Herbert Stein, ed., published monthly (one year, $10; single copy, $1)

Minimum Wage Regulation in Retail Trade, Belton M. Fleisher (129 pp., paper $5.25, cloth $12.25)

Reindustrialization: Boon or Bane? John Charles Daly, mod. (31 pp., $3.75)

Wage Policy in the Federal Bureaucracy, George J. Borjas (59 pp., $4.25)

Minimum Wages, Fringe Benefits, and Working Conditions, Walter J. Wessels (97 pp., $4.25)

Poverty and the Minimum Wage, Donald O. Parsons (62 pp., $4.25)

The Constitution and the Budget, W.S. Moore and Rudolph G. Penner, eds. (172 pp., paper $6.25, cloth $14.25)

Value Added Taxation: The Experience of the United Kingdom, A.R. Prest (52 pp., $4.25)

Money and Liberty, S. Herbert Frankel (67 pp., $4.25)

International Liquidity Issues, Thomas D. Willett (114 pp., $5.25)

Housing: Federal Policies and Programs, John C. Weicher (161 pp., $6.25)

Prices subject to change without notice.

AEI ASSOCIATES PROGRAM

The American Enterprise Institute invites your participation in the competition of ideas through its AEI Associates Program. This program has two objectives:

The first is to broaden the distribution of AEI studies, conferences, forums, and reviews, and thereby to extend public familiarity with the issues. AEI Associates receive regular information on AEI research and programs, and they can order publications and cassettes at a savings.

The second objective is to increase the research activity of the American Enterprise Institute and the dissemination of its published materials to policy makers, the academic community, journalists, and others who help shape public attitudes. Your contribution, which in most cases is partly tax deductible, will help ensure that decision makers have the benefit of scholarly research on the practical options to be considered before programs are formulated. The issues studied by AEI include:

- Defense Policy
- Economic Policy
- Energy Policy
- Foreign Policy
- Government Regulation
- Health Policy
- Legal Policy
- Political and Social Processes
- Social Security and Retirement Policy
- Tax Policy

For more information, write to:

AMERICAN ENTERPRISE INSTITUTE
1150 Seventeenth Street, N.W.
Washington, D.C. 20036